MIGRATION SETTLEMENT AND ETHNIC ASSOCIATIONS

MIGRATION SETTLEMENT AND ETHNIC ASSOCIATIONS

K.P. KUMARAN

CONCEPT PUBLISHING COMPANY, NEW DELHI 110059

ISBN 81-7022-390-3

First Published 1992

Published and Printed by
Ashok Kumar Mittal
Concept Publishing Company
A/15-16, Commercial Block, Mohan Garden
NEW DELHI 110059

Lasertypeset by
Microtech Advance Printing Systems (Pvt.) Ltd.
H-13, Bali Nagar
NEW DELHI 110015

ACKNOWLEDGEMENTS

I have great pleasure in acknowledging my profound gratitude to those who helped me in carrying out this study.

I owe a special debt of gratitude to my teacher and guide Dr. K.S. Nair who supervised this work. I have benefited a lot from him in the form of discussions and invaluable suggestions. It was his constant encouragement and inspiration that helped me to come out with the present text. Thanks are due to Prof. Y.B. Damle, Professor Emiretus, Dr. U.B. Bhoite, Dr. R. Sunder Rajan of Poona University for their help. I am grateful to Prof. Donald V. Kurtz of Wisconsin University, USA, who kindly went through some of the drafts of the thesis and gave valuable suggestions and comments. I also thank Prof. T.K. Oommen and Prof. Sachchidananda for their valuable comments.

A Junior Fellowship was awarded to me by the Anthropological Survey of India, which enabled me to carry out the research work. Thanks to the Survey. I am most grateful to the staff members of Servants of India Society, Pune, Bombay University Library, Bombay, Deccan College Post Graduate and Research Institute and Poona University, Jayakar Library, Pune for the library facilities.

It is not possible for me to list down the names who rendered their sincere help. I owe special thanks to my friends Fr. Johnson, Mr. Rama Rao, Mr. R. Prasannan, Mr. N. Bokhare, and Dr. R.D. Gambhir. Among others it was Sushama Sonak, who took the burden of translating pamphlets and caste journals. I express my sincere gratitude to her. I also take this opportunity to express my deepest feeling of gratitude to my brothers for their constant inspiration, encouragement and support in carrying out the study.

Finally, I will be failing in my duty if I do not express my sincere gratitude to my immigrant friends who provided all necessary help in collecting the data. Among them Mittapalli and Kunden family members deserve special mention.

K.P. KUMARAN

CONTENTS

Acknowledgements 5

List of Maps 8

List of Tables 9

1. Introduction 11
2. Migration and Settlement 37
3. A Typology of Caste Panchayats 55
4. Ethnic Associations and Their Adaptive Functions 91
5. Ethnic Associations and backward Class Movement : A Case Study of Padmasali Sabha 138
6. Conclusions 165

Appendix 175

Bibliography 179

Index 186

LIST OF MAPS

1.1 Map showing Pune Municipal Corporation and Cantonment limits **33**

2.1 Map showing the Settlement areas of the Immigrants during the Pre-colonial period **40**

2.2 Map showing settlement areas of Telugu Immigrant Communities in Pune city and Cantonment area **45**

3.1 Map showing locations of Caste Panchayats **56**

4.1 Map showing locations of active associations **93**

4.2 Map showing locations of passive and disbanded associations **114**

LIST OF TABLES

2.1 Population of Kamaths in the city ot Pune during 1822 **42**

2.2 Classification of Weavers Families by Cast **48**

2.3 South Indian Immigrants in Pune District from 1911 to 1971 **52**

3.1 Comparison of Urban Caste Panchayat with that of village Caste Panchayat **59**

3.2 Classification of Caste Panchayat based on level of organization, level of activity and level of democratization **62**

4.1 Active associations with the Year of Foundation and type **95**

4.2 Distribution of Presidents and Secretaries of Andhra Association on the basis of caste since 1941 **110**

4.3 Passive Associations with the Year of Foundation and Type **113**

4.4 Stages of Transformation, Year of Foundation and Type **125**

4.5 Disbanded Associations along with the year of Foundation, Year of disbandment and type **129**

5.1 Distribution of Padmasalis on the basis of state/region **141**

5.2 Details of Caste Journals **160**

6.1 Comparative Data on characteristics of primary, secondary and modern organization and ethnic associations **170**

1

INTRODUCTION

The Western experience suggests that the proliferation of voluntary associations is the result of urbanization, and it is contended that due to urbanization family, kinship, community and church become weak and the problem of "dehumanization" arise. The proliferation of voluntary associations in the urban area develops in order to compensate the functions of traditional institution. This would mean that as societies become more and more urbanized, the traditional forms of organization are unable to carry out the expected functions and in order to cope with the changing conditions, voluntary associations evolve and develop. The theoretical assumption here is that primary groups are replaced by secondary groups in the urban social structure. Wirth (1938: 22) says: "Being reduced to a stage of virtual impotence as an individual, the urbanite is bound to exert himself by joining with others of similar interest into organized groups to obtain his ends. This results in the enormous multiplication of voluntary organizations. . . ."

The conceptual models of analysis of voluntary associations both in the Western and the African contexts show the functional relationship between voluntary associations and urbanization. In the African context many scholars have noted the birth and proliferation of voluntary associations in relation to the degree of urbanization (Little, 1957; Guy Hunter, 1963; Banton, 1957). Most of the studies on voluntary associations in Africa have stressed the transition of social organization of groups based on ascriptive criteria, such as kinship and tribe, to social organization of groups based on achieved status. Consequently ethnic organizations are also classified into traditional and modern (Little, 1957; Claude Meillassoux, 1968). The basis of such classification can be traced to an evolutionary approach. For instance, Banton (1968) finds an evolutionary approach to voluntary associations more useful in formulating a theory of voluntary associations. Voluntary associations, says Banton, "become common and significant as societies advance in technology, complexity, and scale" (1968 : 588). This shows that in pre-industrial societies the functions of associations are primary in nature and in complex societies it is secondary in nature. The evolutionary approach suggests that when the migrants become more and more advanced or urbanized, the importance of traditional ties based on caste, kinship, region of origin, and language diminishes and that of associations based on occupation, education and income increases. This assumption has led Little (1957), Banton (1968) and Meillassoux (1968) to classify associations into the traditional and the modern.

Some studies on voluntary associations which perform primary as well as secondary group functions are available in the Indian context. Indeed, such associations arise as a response to the process of urbanization. However, voluntary associations proliferate among traditionally based groups in the Indian cities. William Rowe's (1973:408) survey on voluntary associations has shown that many of the associations in Bombay, which are large and affluent enough to have registered offices are specifically organized for the promotion of the welfare of the endogamous groups and the organizational activities are often related to traditionally based groups. The Western experience of urbanization referred to earlier would lead us to believe that with increasing urbanization in India, traditional institutions and values will breakdown. In the Indian urban context this means, among other things, that the caste system would change into a class system, nuclear family would emerge from joint family and the religion would become highly secularized (Rao, 1974:2). But this is not what seems to be happening in India. Urbanization in India may be viewed from a different perspective as, in India, the process of urbanization preceded industrialization and it is not co-terminous with westernisation. In urban India, the migrants settled themselves in ethnic pockets or ghettos. Ethnic segregations have led to the formation of urban villages and these urban villages have some similarities in structure with the rural villages. Studies on family, caste and neighbourhood in the urban context show that with the increasing urbanization, and the concomitant rural to urban migration, the traditional institutions in the cities are not disappearing but are being modified according to the changing situations. (Ames Michael, 1968; Milton Singer, 1968; William Rowe, 1973; Sylvia Vatuk, 1976; A.M. Singh, 1976; Susan Lewandowski, 1978).

The transformation of ethnic organizations from the traditional to the modern as envisaged in the evolutionary approach appears to be not very relevant in the Indian context. A.M. Singh (1976) studied the South Indian immigrants in the city of Delhi with the assumption that both traditional and modern associations exist among them. However, she found no evidence to support the existence of modern organization among this ethnic group. In the conclusion of her study she says: (1976:126) ". . . .it would be entirely inappropriate, in fact to characterize South Indian voluntary associations in Delhi being 'modern' in form and content". The contention of many scholars, especially in the developing countries, is that organizations based on bonds of ethnicity are far more relevant than voluntary associations for the rural migrants in the city.

In the Indian urban context immigrants' associations are mainly formed on the basis of caste, region of origin, language and religion. Prof. Gadgil's (1954) survey in the city of Pune showed an increased strengthening of caste panchayats and communal associations for maintaining identity on the one hand, and for the management of educational and cultural resources on the other. As referred to earlier the associations based on ethnic factors are not disappearing in the Indian context due to urbanization. Traditional associations like caste panchayats are still preserved in the urban setting with some adaptations or modifications in its structure and function. Sangave (1962) studied the changing functions of ten caste organizations ranging from that of Daivadaya Brahmins to the Scheduled Castes of Matangs in the city of Kolhapur and concluded that "The caste Panchayat is preserved in a modified form of introducing the principle of election in constituting the Panchayat or the Managing Committee of the caste, as the case may be" (1962:58).

Some scholars have attempted to distinguish the traditionally based caste panchayats as traditional associations and the recently formed caste sabhas as modern voluntary associations. The function undertaken by several such caste Sabhas was mainly, raising of the social status of the caste group by emulating the twice-born castes. In other words, the main aim was to reform caste customs in the direction of "Sanskritization" and lay claim to higher ranks and to undertake welfare activities. However, in the context of political mobilization and economic development, the main function of these associations is being directed towards political mobilization of caste. This change in function has led to different viewpoints on the nature of these caste Sabhas. One of the view points treats caste Sabhas as voluntary associations and attempts to distinguish traditional caste associations from caste sabhas (Rudolph and Rudolph, 1960; Fox, 1968). The traditional caste associations and the sabhas differ in their function, and also at the organizational level. The caste sabhas resemble, to a certain extent, the voluntary associations that are found in Europe and America. Another and perhaps a more accurate view on caste sabhas is that they are merely an extension of the traditional caste association and that they reflect the enlarged political, economic and social welfare activities of caste (Ghurye, 1961; Srinivas, 1962). Yet another view point has been proposed by Khare (1970) after analysing the caste sabhas of the Kanya Kubja Brahmins of Northern India. He began his research with the assumption that these caste sabhas are modern organizations, but concluded that Kanya Kubja Brahmins sabhas are not purely modern organizations. They are the product of interaction between the traditional and the modern social features and serve specific purposes with specific consequences. In order to underscore the features of the caste sabha he called it as "interjacent organization". A similar conclusion was also drawn by Verma (1979) after studying the caste sabhas of the kurmis in North India.

In the Indian urban context the ethnically based migrant associations do not necessarily turn into the modern voluntary associations. Therefore, dichotomization of ethnic associations into the traditional and the modern appears to be inappropriate. The structure of these associations may appear to be modern on account of registration, presence of office, introduction of democratic principles and the changing functions. Insofar as the basis of recruitment of members in these associations is based on certain ascriptive criteria, such as caste, language, region of origin and religion, and their functions are limited to the ethnic groups, it is not appropriate to treat them as voluntary associations. In a multiethnic country like India, associations which are formed on the basis of ethnicity may be called ethnic associations rather than voluntary associations. In the present context associations which are formed on the basis of ethnicity are considered as ethnic associations. The changes that are observed in the structure and function may be viewed simply as a part of the process of adaptation. Since India is considered to be one of the biggest transitional societies, of course, the traditional and the modern elements do co-exist in various types of ethnic associations. In order to understand these changes the emphasis ought to be on structural and functional adaptations of ethnic associations from a historical perspective. In the present context ethnic associations have been analysed from this perspective.

THE PROBLEM

I

Broadly speaking the aim of this research is to assess the role of ethnic associations in the process of urbanization. As in the case of Western and African urbanization, the Indian process of urbanization has also led to the proliferation of voluntary associations. However, despite urbanization, the traditional institutions are preserved in the cities by the immigrants through their associations formed on the basis of their ethnicity. At the outset the present study attempts a historical analysis of migration and settlement of the immigrants in an Indian city in order to ascertain whether there is any co-relation between proliferation of ethnic associations and the process of urbanization.

II

Among the immigrants various types of associations develop during the various stages of the development of the ethnic community. In India, literature on ethnic associations shows that with the increasing urbanization, industrialization, and the concomitant large-scale rural to urban migration, the associations which are formed on the basis of ethnicity do not transform into modern voluntary associations with secondary relations among its members. This raises the question that if they are not transforming into secondary associations, what is actually happening to them? Do they die off once the intended function is over? Do they progress over time on a scale of tradition to modern? What kinds of structural and functional changes do they undergo in the context of rapid urbanization and industrialization? In order to answer these questions the present study enquires into the nature of the structural and functional adaptation or modifications that these associations have undergone in the urban context from a historical perspective. Based on the nature and degree of the structural and functional adaptation that several ethnic associations have undergone over time, a taxonomy of ethnic association has also been attempted in this study.

III

In the African context numerous studies on the role of voluntary associations as adaptive and adjustment mechanisms in the process of urbanization are available. (Clement, 1956; Little, 1965; Lloyd, 1967; Plotnicov, 1967; Meillassoux, 1968; Kerri, 1972). These studies have stressed the extent to which these associations perform primary group functions, which help the migrants to adapt and adjust to the changing urban conditions. Little Kenneth (1965) in his pioneering work "West African Urbanization: A Study of Voluntary Associations in Social Change" showed that voluntary associations perform adaptive and adjustment functions by facilitating the process of grafting rural migrants on to the social life of towns and cities. They are also found to fulfil wide ranging functions from tribal identity reinforcement to mutual aid. However, Sheldon (1976) has pointed out the changing roles of ethnic associations in the African context. According to him the role of regional clubs during the initial stages of migration is "informal buffer" or adaptive and during later stages its function becomes purely recreational. This would mean that the functions of ethnic associations change to expressive from instrumental once the migrants have established themselves in the city. He further states that the club is neither a rural enclave in the city nor a truly urban institution, but a temporary phase in the process of urbanization. In the western context also a similar view has been expressed by Cutler (1973:55). He says: The primary associations have become less useful as integrative mechanisms in America as the population has improved its standard of living. In the west African context also (Barnes and Peil, 1977:85) showed this tendency, even though the standard of living of the urban population is comparatively low. Adaptive and adjustment functions of ethnic associations appear to be limited to the early stages of migration and settlement.

In the Indian context as well ethnic associations have been studied with some reference to their adaptive and adjustment functions (Rowe, 1973; A.M. Singh, 1975; Nair, 1978; Susan Lewandowski, 1980). These studies have shown that ethnic associations render primary group functions to the migrants through various socio-cultural activities. Participation in these ethnic associations helped the migrants to have face-to-face contact and hence highly personalized interpersonal interactions. Anderson and Anderson (1962:168) show three kinds of bonds which unite the individuals into the social groups in the urban context: they are kinship, locality and shared interest. Ethnic background variables such a language, region of origin, religion and caste have been stressed by several authors as the basis of formation of ethnic associations in the Indian cities (Punekar, 1975; Nair, 1978). Associations based on these factors have been widely reported in the literature on the ethnic association in the Indian urban context.

Migration and settlement in Indian cities shows that migrants who came from a particular region settled in a particular locality in order to promote the traditional cultural environment. Replication of the traditional cultural environment provides a cushioning effect to the cultural shock arising out of contact with other cultures. In order to explain the above mentioned role of ethnic association, Nair (1978) used the "Simulation" model. This model suggests that immigrant's native culture and structure are simulated in the city through the activities of ethnic associations. Simulation model does not envisage exact replication of the native culture and structure, but provides for certain functional adaptation in both culture and structure.

A few studies on ethnic associations in the Indian context also deal with the role of the associations in ethnic identity maintenance of the immigrants. Participation in ethnic associational activities have been found to enhance the ethnic identity of the immigrants. De Witt John (1963:39) noted that "immigrant associations might also act as symbols of unity and identity of the immigrant community". Although some studies on ethnic associations in the Indian context, which stress on their adaptive and integrative functions are available, systematic studies on how these associations act as adaptive and adjustment mechanisms to the immigrants in the city, during the various stages of development of the immigrant communities are not available. Therefore, in the present study the following questions have been raised: (1) To what extent are these associations acting as adaptive mechanisms or "informal buffer" for the immigrants in the city with special reference to primary group activities? (2) Whether these associations continuously act as adaptive mechanism or "informal buffer" to the immigrants? If not to what extent do these associations change their structure and functions over-time? (3) To what extent ethnic associations are helpful in preserving the identity of the immigrants in the city, and in what way?

IV

The role of ethnic associations in the context of political modernization and economic development is another important area of inquiry. For the last few decades caste associations have been proliferating in the Indian context as a response to the modern political culture. For a long time the tendency was for castes to divide themselves into endogamous group for the sake of social mobility. This fissiparous tendency is replaced by the amalgamation of analogous caste with a view to the exercise of social and political influence (Hutton, 1946:45). These larger amalgamated bodies presented by the caste associations have been regarded as the adaptive response to the modern conditions of pluralistic democracy (Rudolph and Rudolph, 1960:15). This unification of endogamous caste leads to competitive nature of caste in Indian politics. Caste associations have been known to act as a vehicle for the social mobility of the caste through the process of "Sanskritisation". After Independence the mobility for status through the process of Sanskritisation is being replaced by a horizontal solidarity of caste groups to demand various facilities that are available to the lower caste groups in the Constitution. The policy of "protective discrimination" has led the lower caste groups to desanskritising themselves in order to be categorized in the Backward Caste List and to demand the reservation facilities that are available to the Scheduled Caste and Tribe Communities.

Therefore, in this work, with the help of case study we attempt to explore the role of caste sabhas in the Backward Classes movement. We intend to study the development of caste sabhas from a historical perspective in order to understand the changes that had taken place in their functions, organizational set up, objectives, and leadership pattern.

THEORETICAL PERSPECTIVE

Mass migration of people to cities leads to the formation of group settlement in certain ecological niches. The literature on group settlement in the western context shows that ties of kinship, common culture, neighbourliness, village or district allegiance act as the basis for the group settlement of immigrants in the city. (C.A. Galitzi, 1929:88; Belegan, 1940; Yuzyk, 1953). Group settlement in certain geographical area helped the immigrants to form ethnic communities and ethnic associations in the city. The pattern of group settlement may vary according to the nature of migration, and this, in turn, may have a bearing on the nature ethnic associations. It may, therefore, be worthwhile to explore the possible relationship between the nature of associations formed and various types of migration and settlement from a historical perspective.

Group Settlement and Ethnic Associations

The relationship between the type of migration and pattern of settlement has been forwarded by Price (1959:27). He classified group settlement patterns into three types on the basis of the type of migration. They are:

(1) Organized group settlement;
(2) Chain settlement; and
(3) Gravitation group settlement.

Organized group settlement was widely seen all over the world during the pre-industrial period. This type of settlement is founded by organized religious refugees or they are formed when groups of labourers are brought in order to develop a particular area. The best example for the organised group settlement is that of plantation workers or coolies in the African countries and the South East Asian countries. Based on the duration of stay in a particular area, the organized group settlement can be divided into two: Permanent settlement and Temporary settlement. The settlement of Indian coolies in Africa in order to replace or supplement the Negro labourers on the sugar plantations during the eighteenth century is an example of organized permanent settlement (Kondapi, 1951; Saha, 1970; Tinker, 1974). The contract labourers or "indentured labourers" settlements are of a temporary nature and they fall into the second category . The settlements of migrant labourers from India to the Middle East where the labourers are assigned to work in certain areas on the basis of certain contract are examples of temporary settlements. Once the contract is over the labourers usually return to their native place. The migration and settlement in this case is of a temporary nature. However, a small group of migrants who choose to settle down while many others return, may provide the nucleaus for the formation of ethnic groups through other patterns of migration and settlement such as chain migration and gravitational settlement.

Another form of migration influencing the development of ethnic concentration in the cities is chain migration. Chain migration is a process whereby new immigrants are brought to the cities by friends and relatives who have already migrated and settled in the cities. This type of migration and group settlement have been noted by many scholars (Glass, 1960; MacDonald and MacDonald, 1964; Jones, 1964; Hiro, 1971). Chain migration is a continuous process whereby migrants attract the new immigrants through a chain of letters and other contacts. Chain settlements are stronger in comparison to the organized group settlements, since the chain moves on the basis of less formal relationships of kinship and friendship.

A gravitational group settlement is formed when groups of people who have migrated independently to cities, attract each other to form a common settlement. The forces which attract them to form settlements are common culture, language, customs and religion. This type of settlement has also been reported by many scholars (Blegan, 1940; Park, 1955; and Hiro, 1971).

Price (1959:271) has explicitly taken into consideration the dynamics of group settlement in his three-fold classification of group settlement patterns. However, he has mentioned that these three-fold settlement pattern need not retain their original character. The existing model which explains the aftermath changes that are involved in ethnic group settlement is that of dispersal model. Dispersal model suggests that there is a dispersal of residential segregation as well as a breakdown of ethnic groups by assimilating the immigrants into the host society. In the American context, the dispersal of ethnic concentration and ethnic group is considered as a gradual process. During the initial stages of migration, immigrants tend to segregate in compact colonies. Once they improve their economic and social standing the immigrants move out of their old residence to a lesser physically concentrated locality. Once the immigrants acquire standards of living similar to those of the members of the host society, the residential segregation is expected to disperse, and consequently the ethnic group is assimilated into the mainstream (Cressey 1938:61).

The dispersal model of immigrants settlement is essentially an outgrowth of the concept of assimilation and melting pot which were prevalent in the western context for a long time. The concept of assimilation and melting pot were questioned by many scholars even though the concept may be partially applicable to explain American society. Various studies have shown that the dispersal of residential segregation of ethnic groups do not call for the complete assimilation of ethnic groups (Banton 1955; Borleks 1970). Even if there is a dispersal of ethnic group, ethnic identity is preserved by various ethnic associations. Etzioni (1959:258) stressed that group identity is not maintained by concentration in certain residential areas, but through the sentiments and interests based on past experience, education, and communication. This common bond is reinforced through ethnic newspapers, organizations, clubs and synagogues where members meet, even though they do not live next to each other and are not concentrated in one ecological area. The dispersed immigrants may maintain their contracts with the original settlement through participation in the various associations which have already been formed. Therefore, through participation in various ethnic associations, immigrants preserve their ethnic identity inspite of ethnic desegregation.

Ethnic segregation resulting from the settlement of immigrants in the cities has influenced the nature and form of associations. During the initial stages of migration and settlement it has been widely noted by many scholars that immigrants tend to form associations mainly on the basis of ethnicity in order to adapt themselves to the city life. Such associations formed during the migration and settlement helped the immigrants to have informal or less formal relations and they satisfy to a large extent their socio-cultural and, to some extent, economic needs. Many authors in the western context content that the associations formed during the initial stage of migration and settlement do not retain their adaptive and adjustment functions. As the immigrants are well-settled or adapted to the life of the host society, the adaptive and adjustment functions are transformed.

The dynamics of group settlement and the consequent changes in structure and function of ethnic associations may be posited if we analyse the types of migration and settlement and ethnic associations in Indian cities from a historical perspective. Migration and urbanization to Indian cities started even before the onset of industrialization. While studying urbanization in the Indian context one has to stress the traditional or precolonial urbanization. Migration and settlement in the Indian cities can be categorized roughly into three periods. They are: (1) pre-colonial, (2) colonial, and (3) post-colonial.

Urbanization during the Pre-colonial Period

During the pre-colonial period pilgrims moved in groups to the religious centres which in the Indian context were administrative and religious cities. Pilgrims had very minimal contact with the host society by their isolating themselves from the host society. In the context of migration of pilgrims to the religious centres H. Acharya (1969:62) says that pilgrims hardly had any contact and minimal interaction with the host society because of their language, culture, and customs differed from those of the host society. Such a situation enhanced the formation of ethnic segregation as well as ethnic communities during the pre-colonial period. Similarly artisans, skilled craftsmen, and scavengers from villages moved to the city capitals to work as labourers, on construction, and in sanitary services. Many of them were repatriated once the intended work was over. This type of migration is similar to the contract or "indentured" labour migration which is prevalent in the Middle East countries today. Labourers are taken to cities on the basis of contract to work for five to ten years. They may be under the custody of some governmental or private agencies. Once the contract work was over many of them went back to their native places. In the cities, even though they are under the custody of some employer or governmental agencies, their interaction is mainly directed to the urban villages or those castes who have similar ethnic characteristics. The segregation of ethnic groups and the minimum interaction and contact with the host society lead to the formation of ethnic communities and ethnic associations during the pre-colonial period.

As the people migrated to the cities they lost most of their direct contact with their kindred and neighbourhood of origin. In order to compensate for the primary needs which were once met by the village community or kith and kin, immigrants formed associations on the basis of informal relations. As Meillassoux (1968:24) puts it: "The prime need of the new city dweller is to set himself into a system of collective security comparable to that which was provided by the rural society". The associations which are formed on the basis of ethnic ties continue to act as adaptive and adjustive mechanisms by providing a traditional environment where he spend most of his life. In other words, they provide "a stable base for traditionalists resident in a non-traditional milieu" (Anderson, 1971:217). During the pre-colonial period the chances of formation of ethnic associations were rather few. Even if the associations were formed, they were only for a temporary period. The settlements were not always permanent as the original settlers often went back to their native place, once the intended purpose of migration has been served. The ethnic group as well as the associations disappear as the migrants return to their native place.

Urbanization During the Colonial Period

Even though urbanization was "situational" during the pre-colonial period a few immigrants remained in the cities if the conditions were favourable for them. They further attracted their relatives and friends or villagers to migrate to cities. Chain migration and settlement intensified during the colonial era. During the colonial period new industries were established by the British in big cities like Bombay, Calcutta, and Madras. Introduction of communication system and easy means of transport enabled the immigrants to move to industrial and administrative centres in search of employment. This enhanced the flow of new immigrants to the cities and new settlements were formed. Some settlements became stronger and others flexible. Because of these facilities the settlements which were formed during the pre-colonial period also expanded due to the further action of chain migration.

The associations which were formed during the pre-colonial era became permanent in nature. In addition to old associations new associations were also formed in order to meet the demands of new immigrants. The settlements became stronger since the settlers were mainly from a particular caste or village. They simulated the culture of the place of origin by developing various types of associations which were more or less similar to traditional associations back home. The associations formed on the basis of chain migration and settlement were stronger because the people who settled on the basis of chain migration were channelized on the basis of kinship, friendship, caste or village. Since the immigrants were from the same caste or village it paved the way for them to have informal interpersonal relations by forming various types of ethnic associations. At this stage caste panchayats similar to those of the village caste panchayats were also formed by the immigrants in the cities. The functions of these associations were directed towards the adaptive and adjustive functions and to some extent to satisfy the emotional needs of the members by performing the role of primary groups.

In addition to chain migration and settlement the gravitational group settlements were also widely observed in the Indian cities during the colonial era. Rural to urban and inter regional migrations also strengthened at this stage. People from villages as well as different cultural regions were recruited in the British armed forces for various services. People who were employed in the military services were forced to move to different parts of the country along with the military regiment during times of war. When a war was over, a few members went back to their native places, some settled in cantonment areas, others where the regiment was disbanded. People who came along with the military regiment as well as those who migrated individually in search of employment and had similar culture, language or caste status attracted one another to settle in one particular ecological region. Since the number of immigrants from the caste or village was comparatively small, it necessitated the immigrants to settle on a broader ethnic factors like language, common culture, or common caste status. This facilitated the formation of caste federations during the colonial era. Various castes or communities came together and formed caste federations in order to adapt and adjust themselves to city life. In addition to primary functions like security, mutual aid the federation also fulfilled the immigrant's socio-cultural and religious needs, thereby integrating whole communities under one banner.

The formation of caste federations during the colonial period is parallel to the caste federations that are seen in contemporary India. In contemporary India studies have shown that there is a tendency for castes of similar status and interest to come together to form caste federations for a common goal or objectives. But many political scientists have shown that formation of caste federations are for the political mobilization of caste in order to acquire power (Rudolph and Rudolph 1965; Gough 1965; Kothari and Maru 1965; Weiner 1967). But during the colonial era formation of caste federations were to facilitate the immigrant's adaptation and adjustment to the city or rather for the survival of immigiants in the city.

The types of associations that are formed on the basis of gravitation and chain settlement should be distinguished at this stage. The immigrants who settled in one locality on the basis of chain migration are more or semi related on the basis of kinship, friendship, village or caste. This helped immigrants to have more informal relationships among themselves. Moreover, the associations that are formed may be strong as well as lasting. In the case of gravitational group settlement, on the other hand, the members are not related on the basis of caste or village or friendship. Naturally the associations were formed on a broader ethnic factor like common culture or language or common status. So the associations which are formed may not be as strong as those seen in chain settlement.

During the initial stages, caste federation was helpful as an adaptive and adjustment mechanism for the immigrants. But once the immigrants are well settled in the city there may be a tendency for the immigrants to split off from the federation on the basis of caste or village in order to have their own associations. Mangin (1959:207) described the type of fission of regional associations among the Ancash clubs in Peru. He says: "when a club reaches certain size and age, roughly between 50 to 150 members and from 2 to 10 years, there is a tendency toward factional splitting. Sometimes these splits are based on local kinship or social class line, sometimes they are political, but more commonly they are associated with personality clashes within the lima". Fusion and fission of association and the partial dispersal of ethnic concentration are mainly associated with gravitational group settlement. Fission of associations and the partial dispersal of ethnic concentration are rarely seen in chain group settlement.

Urbanization During Post-colonial Period

During the post colonial era the influx of immigrants increased in tc Indian cities considerably. Industrialization was one of the reasons, for it opened new avenues for employment for the immigrants. This intensified the interregional and rural to urban migration. The main types of migration in this stage are individual and chain migration. The people who migrated during the colonial and pre-colonial era were mainly lower caste communities. In the villages the lower caste community members were under the control of caste panchayats. When they were released from the custodian of traditional caste panchayats, immigrants tended to form caste panchayats in the cities similar to that of village in order to enjoy similar functions hitherto rendered by the village caste panchayats. Thus during the pre-colonial and colonial period this was one of the reasons lower caste communities clustered together in certain ecological areas.

During the post colonial period the ethnic concentrations that were formed during the colonial and pre-colonial era started growing and got saturated. The new immigrants were not able to find places to live in the old residential areas. Many people immigrated at this stage on account of job transfers or new appointment and were of the educated class. Since the old settlement area was saturated, people started settling down wherever accommodation was available. Many immigrants were compelled to scatter all over the city because of lack of accommodations. New settlements were also formed on the basis of gravitational group settlement in outskirts of the city. Even people who have acquired money and status started moving away from the old settlements to new places. This may be for better housing and amenities. Settlement on the basis of class level can also be seen at this stage. This type of partial dispersal of ethnic concentration in Indian cities does not lead to the total dispersal of ethnic segregation or assimilation of ethnic groups. Even though there is a partial dispersal of ethnic concentration the ethnic identity of immigrants is preserved by participating in various types of associations. Many of the associations which were formed during the pre-colonial and colonial period may survive even today without having any substantial structural and functional change. Some associations have died out once their intended functions were over. Still others might have undergone structural and functional adaptations in order to meet the changing needs of city life. New associations were also formed in order to meet the changing needs of the immigrants.

The hypothesis regarding types of migration, settlement and the formation of association leads us to search a model for the analysis of ethnic associations in the urban setting. Many anthropologists in the African and western contexts analysed ethnic associations in terms of an evolutionary model of society. Banton (1968) and Kerri (1974) stated that when society changes from a pre-industrial society to a bureaucratized impersonalised industrial society, the functions of ethnic associations also change. It is assumed that in cities due to industrialization and urbanization, the traditional associations based on primary ties quickly become inappropriate and new associational forms develop. This assumption led various scholars in the African context to classify ethnic associations into traditional and modern (Little, 1965; Meillassoux, 1968). The transformation or replacement of associations based on primary ties to secondary ties is not taking place in the Indian urban context. As referred to earlier, studies focussing on caste, kinship and descent showed that with increasing industrialization and urbanization the traditional institutions are not disappearing or breaking down, but undergo adaptive modification. These studies have also shown that voluntary associations are not acting as a substitute for, or replacing, the traditional forms of solidarities. So a classification of ethnic associations into traditional and modern as envisaged in the western and African contexts may not be applicable in the Indian context.

In the present study we have analysed the ethnic associations on the basis of structure and function. The changes or modifications that are observed in the structure and function of the association are considered as adaptations to cope with the changing urban scene. Structural and functional adaptation may be defined as changes or modifications in ethnic associations during various stages of their development in order to cope with changing conditions. In order to study the structural development three components of structure are considered: level of organization, level of activity and level of democratization. Wunsch (1978) had used these factors for measuring the structural development of voluntary associations in the West African context. However, in the present study, the parameters for measuring the three levels of structure have been used with certain modifications.

Level of Organization

The following indicators have been used to study the level of organization: (i) record keeping; (ii) written rules and regulations; (iii) defined procedure for selecting office bearers; (iv) defined decision making processes; (v) specified meetings; (vi) specified organizational activity; (vii) defined criteria for membership; and (viii) registration of organization.

Level of Activity

Activity is measured in terms of the following indicators: (i) presence of general body meeting; (ii) committee meetings; (iii) collection of membership fees; (iv) exercise of a common property; and (v) exercise of a common fund.

Level of Democratization

Democratization is measured in terms of the following indicators:

(1) Initial selection of office bearers by election;
(2) Participation of members in election;
(3) Regular election;
(4) General participation in decision-making; and
(5) Division of labour among office bearers.

Ethnic Associations and Backward Class Movement*

Caste sabhas play a major role in raising the social and economic status of caste members. This is achieved by adopting certain methods in different time periods. Generally speaking, the Backward caste movement in India passed through two stages. The first one was through the processes of Sanskritisation in order to acquire the status of the twice born caste. Prof. M.N. Srinivas (1956) introduced the concept of "Sanskritisation" and "Westernisation" for the aspiration of upward mobility. Various studies have shown that through Sanskritisation the lower caste emulated the customs, habits and manners of the upper caste in a quest for status rather than power. As noted by Srinivas (1972), so long as the traditional norms of Hindu society were dominant and preserved by upper castes, Sanskritisation was the only and also natural means for upward socio-cultural mobility. The widespread mobility of Backward castes was reported during the years 1867-1871, when the First National Census was undertaken. Two Tamil peasant castes, Vellalas and Padaiyachis from Tamil Nadu demanded that they should be recorded, as belonging to a higher varna. The Vellalas were included among the Shudras and wanted to be classed as Vaishyas, and Padaiyachis wanted to be classed as Vanniya-Kula Kshatriyas.

For a long time caste sabhas played a pivotal role in accelerating the social mobility of caste members by reforming the caste customs, (e.g., stressing education of women, remarriage of widows, curtailment of marriage expenses, etc.). This aspiration continued till the early decades of the twentieth century.

The second emphasis on mobility is for higher status through the allocation of political power. In contemporary India, proliferation of caste sabhas is a response to the changing political and economic conditions. Today the main function of caste sabhas is to mobilize caste members politically to acquire political power. After independence, in the Constitution, various facilities are conferred on the backward communities in the field of education, job, administration and politics. The emergence of caste sabha in order to acquire these

* The backward classes are broadly classified into three categories. They are scheduled castes, scheduled tribes and the other backward classes. In the present study we are dealing with the third category, who are considered as low level Hindu caste and entitled to economic and educational privileges from the Government.

facilities is worth noting. Now the tendency of social mobility through Sanskritisation is minimized; instead there is a horizontal movement of lower caste communities to organize themselves as caste associations in order to maintain their identity on the one hand, and, on the other, to demand the Constitutional and democratic rights. Yogendra Singh (1973:171) puts it thus: "Earlier aspiration for vertical mobility or Sanskritisation among the lower castes has now been replaced by a new feeling of self identity within one's own caste or increased horizontal caste solidarity. Caste associations are an indirect reflection of this new trend".

Since independence caste has entrenched itself more strongly than ever. The policy of protective discrimination led the lower caste communities to change the mobility pattern. In Mysore, the Backward Class Committee excluded the powerful Lingayat caste from the Backward class list in 1961 and the repercussion was intense political campaigning in order to put them into the backward class list.

Scheme of the Thesis

The thesis is divided into six major chapters. The first chapter is divided into two parts. The first part deals with the research questions and the theoretical framework. The theoretical models which have been developed in the western and African contexts for the analysis of ethnic associations and its applicability in the Indian urban situation have been critically evaluated. Many scholars have noted that associations formed on the basis of ethnicity as voluntary associations. However, in the present study it is argued that insofar as the basis of recruitment of members in these associations is based on ethnic principles like caste, language, region of origin and religion and their functions are limited to ethnic groups, it is not appropriate to treat them as voluntary associations. A model for the analysis of ethnic associations in the Indian urban context has been proposed. The process of Indian urbanization is studied with particular reference to Pune city. The dynamic relationship among types of migration, settlement and the types of associations are also postulated in this part. The second part deals with research methodology, and details out methods, techniques and tools used in this study.

Chapter 2 provides a brief description of each community under study and provides the historical background of their imigration and settlement. Migration and settlement have been analysed in three time periods. They are pre-colonial, colonial and post-colonial. This part also explores the possible relationship among the types of migration and settlement and the nature of ethnic association which are formed in the process of migration and settlement. Apart from identifying the types of migration and settlement, the basis of settlement is also explored in this chapter.

Chapter 3 provides a model to analyse ethnic associations in the Indian urban context. Data have shown that the existing model of analysis of ethnic associations in the African and Western contexts is not appropriate in the Indian urban context, and they have further shown that association based on primary ties are neither transforming nor are they replaced by secondary ties. Instead they are undergoing structural and functional adaptations. So 20 caste panchayats have been analysed extensively in order to study the structural and functional adaptations undergone by them over time. Based on the structural and functional adaptations a typology of caste panchayat has beer attempted. They are fused, transitional differentiated.

Chapter 4 deals with the changing role of ethnic associations over time. Analyses show that according to the need structure of the immigrant communities, various associations are formed by them. During the initial stages of migration and settlement the associations formed by them are adaptive and adjustment in their function, which helped the rural migrants to graft on to the city. The associations which are formed on a later stage are mainly of integrative, identity maintenance and social welfare oriented in their functions. Immigrants form certain associations in the city in order to attain certain goals. Once the intended function of the associations is achieved, they may become passive or disappear or transform into another form. Considering the structural and functional adaptations undergone by ethnic associations, they have been classified into four categories. They are active, passive, transformed and disbanded. Associations have been analysed historically and numerous factors responsible for the activity, passivity, transformation and disbandment of ethnic associations are identified in this Chapter.

Chapter 5 examines the dynamic role played by ethnic associations in the Backward classes movement. The various strategies adopted by them for the social mobility of lower class communities are dealt with in detail. Until the beginning of the 20th century the lower caste communities were trying to emulate the social status of the twice born castes through the process of sanskritisation to demand a high social status. Especially after Independence owing to the government's policy of "protective discrimination" a reverse process of Sanskritisation, that is "desanskritisation" is prevalent among them in order to demand the various facilities conferred on them in the field of education, occupation and politics. The present data show that both types of mobility exist among immigrant communities. The dynamic role played by ethnic associations in order to facilities the both types of movement has been analysed in detail.

The concluding chapter highlights the important findings of this study.

THE METHODOLOGY

The Setting of the Study

Pune is pleasantly situated at a height of about 1,850 ft. above the sea level at the confluence of the Mula and the Mutha, two of the countless riverlets that originate in the western ghats. Pune city is the head-quarters of Pune district in the State of Maharashtra, India. It is situated in 18° 31′ N and 73° 51′ E and is on the Central Railway, 190 km. southeast of Bombay.

Pune is endowed with an excellent climate, and is popularly known as the centre for retired people. It has a mean rainfall of 26.63" with 48 rainy days on an average. Pune has a hot season from March to May, and a wet season from June to October.

Historical Background of the City

The importance of Pune commenced at the time of Baji Rao Peshwa I, who started construction of the city around A.D. 1721, in order to make it suitable for the city capital of the Marathas. As early as 1734, he had constructed the first ward, Shukrawar peth in Pune. Following Baji Rao Peshwa, Nana Peshwa had founded two more wards. They are, Guruwar and Vetal peths. By the end of Peshwa's rule in Pune, there were twenty wards. After the capture of Pune by the Britishers, in 1817, the Pune and Kirkee Cantonments were formed. The Pune Municipality came into existence in the year 1856. On 15th Feb. 1950 Pune Municipality has been raised to the status of Municipal Corporation. Since the 1950s new industries have sprang up in the city as well as in the sub-urban areas. Today Pune is a fast industrializing city. Three new industrial belts have been formed in the outskirts of the city recently. In 1970 Pune was divided into 73 wards. Map 1.1. shows Pune Municipal Corporation and Cantonment limits along with the main peths formed by the Peshwa.

The early immigrants who came from Nizambad dominion during the middle of the 18th Century settled in the wards of Shukrawar Peth, Vetal and Ganj. During the initial stages of the British regime in Pune, the immigrants who came along with the British regiment settled mainly at the Pune Cantonment and a few at the Kirkee Cantonment. On a later stage, the Telugu immigrants encroached on various other parts of the city. During the pre-colonial and colonial period, settlement was mainly at a certain geographical area, and the immigrants were restricted to certain caste groups. During the post colonial period immigrant settlements is rather scattered and is without special reference to any particular locality. The Telugu immigrant communities under study live mainly in the wards of Bhavanipeth, Nanapeth, Rasthapeth, Ghorpadi, Kirkee and Pune Camp. The details of their settlement are given in the next chapter with maps.

Methods of Data Collection

For a long time primitive and peasant societies were considered as Anthropologists major field of study and analysis. Recently an increasing number of Anthropologists have become interested in studying the various complex societies. Numerous scholars have supported the view that when we shift our study from a culturally homogeneous society to a more complex and heterogeneous society, the tool and methods also should be changed (Steward, 1967; Despress, 1968). Herbert Gans (1962) studied the urban neighbourhood in Boston and showed that, in the city urban villages also are seen, and they have many of the characteristics of village life, such as primary group relationships, informal interpersonal relationships, and social cohesion. As the people migrate to cities, the traditional mode of sodalities are not given up completely. In addition to the traditional sodalities, new forms of relationships are also developed in the cities by the immigrants in order to promote adaptation and adjustment to the city life. In the present context, our interest is mainly to study how associations which provide for primary ties are helpful to the immigrants in adjusting and adapting to the city life. Therefore, it is justifiable to use the traditional ethnographic methods with slight

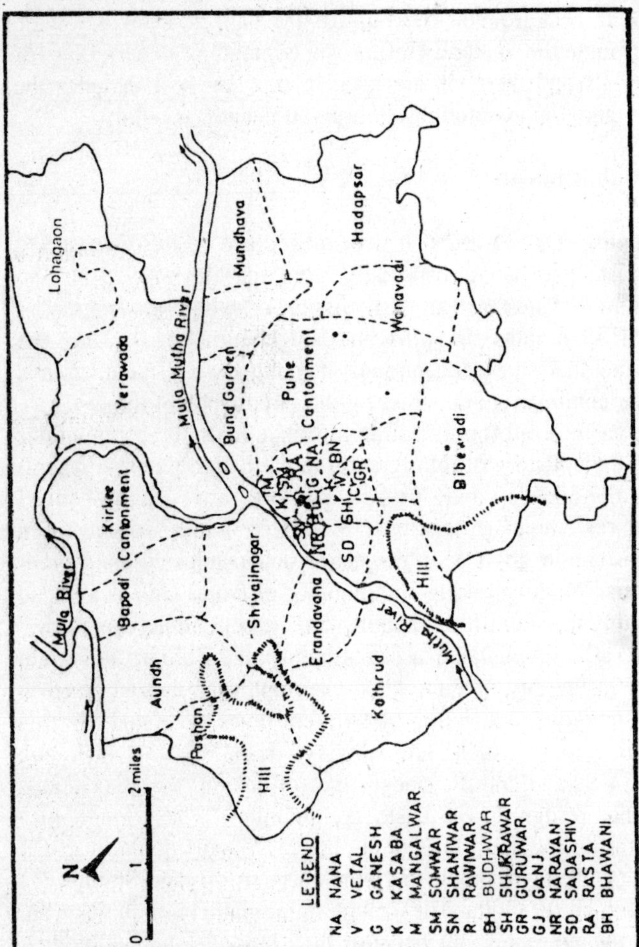

MAP 1.1: Map showing Pune Municipal Corporation and Cantonment limits

modification, in the urban setting in order to study the dynamism of organisational activity as well as organizational life. Moreover, the communities under study represent homogeneous group at least in terms of ethnic background. The bulk of the data in this study were collected through the method of urban ethnography. A variety of source materials and methods are used in this study. It includes the methods of ethnographic interviews observation and case study.

Rapport Establishment

In the beginning stages I found it very difficult to collect data on the traditional caste panchayats especially from the elderly persons. So during the initial stages instead of focussing on ethnic associations, I had spent few months in different neighbourhoods (where the community members are concentrated) meeting the old members and leaders of the community and stressing the importance of the research. This period was utilized for collecting information on the communities in general and the history of immigration in particular. Later on when I won their confidence and proper rapport was established, I concentrated on ethnic associations. Moreover, while working as a research assistant in an ICSSR project, I had conducted field work among various Telugu speaking communities of Pune. This fact helped me considerably in establishing rapport with the community members.

Data on all the available associations of the Telugu immigrant communities in the city of Pune have been collected and analysed in this study. Numerous association of different types were studied. This include associations which are already dead, those which are transformed, weakend and disbanded. Except one, all the associations belong to the Telugu lower caste communities. The communities studied are the following: (1) Padmasali; (2) Telugu Mannurwar; (3) Telugu Nai; (4) Telugu Dhobi; (5) Mannewar; (6) Telugu Shimpi; (7) Telugu Mochi and (8) Golla. The Telugu immigrant communities were selected for the present study because they have a long tradition of migration to Pune, they have got maximum number of associations, and they dominate in population more than any other south Indian immigrants to the city of Pune. Major part of the data for the fifth chapter have been collected from Bombay and Sholapur. Moreover, this part has been substantiated with adequate secondary sources.

Methods of Interview

Two types of interviews have been used to collect data from ethnic associations. They are individual and group interviews. In each association, all the office bearers were interviewed individually. In order to cross check the information, group interviews were also conducted. The groups included a few members as well as the office bearers. In certain cases, especially that of caste panchayat, office bearers, were not ready to provide detailed information individually. In such cases, whatever information that was available collected from them individually. Further, group interviews were conducted to supplement the information. The group included members in addition to the office bearers. Ex-office bearers were also interviewed in order to get the past histories of the association. Elderly persons in the community were contacted to obtain historical data about the community.

A detailed interview guide was prepared in order to collect data on the genesis, growth and development of ethnic associations, during the various stages of their development. The following information have been collected from each association:

1. Genesis and growth, major accomplishment and major changes over the years;
2. Criteria of membership, its ethnic, educational and occupational characteristics;
3. Details of meetings, and functions organized by each association and the cultural, social and public events, arranged by them;
4. Participation of members and office bearers in meeting and functions arranged by each association;
5. Source of income, annual income, annual expenditure of each association; and
6. Written or printed rules and regulations of each association.

Observation

During the field work, I made use of all the opportunities to attend the meetings and functions arranged by most of the associations. Quasi-participant observational technique was used to collect information about the community life in general and in particular the activities arranged by each association. Almost all secondary data on ethnic associations were collected from available sources, such as documents, souveniers, notices, annual records, pamphlets and the like.

Analysis and Presehtation of Data

Data on 71 Ethnic associations have been collected as case studies and presented in this work. Out of the 71 associations include 20 caste panchayats, 28 Active associations, three passive associations, one Transformed association and six Disbanded associations. Another 13 associations are caste sabhas. Most of the caste sabhas are functioning at state level. Even though data on all the 71 associations have been collected in detail, in certain cases only representative cases from each type have been described in detail.

2

MIGRATION AND SETTLEMENT

Migration is generally classified into two categories: (1) voluntary, and (2) forced or impelled migration. In this work a few cases of forced migration are reported; they are cases of those who left their native place because of natural calamities like famine and epidemics, but their number is very few. So, in the present study, the type of migration of Telugu speaking people to the city of Pune is generally considered as voluntary. Numerous castes and community members from Andhra Pradesh migrated individually, as well as in groups, and settled in various parts of Pune city, during different chronological periods. During the initial stage of migration it was the lower caste members who dominated in number, and at later stages most of the immigrants were educated and members of the upper and middle caste. It is said that migration and settlement of Telugu speaking people started even during the period of Shivaji, however, no valid documents are available to substantiate this view. In the present context, migration and settlement of Telugu speaking people to the city of Pune is divided into three periods: They are (1) pre-colonial period, (2) colonial period, and (3) post-colonial period.

Pre-colonial period

The first phase of migration of Telugu speaking people to the city of Pune started in the early decades of eighteenth century during the time of the Peshwa's dynasty. At this period it was mainly lower caste groups that migrated to Pune. They were popularly known as "Kamathis". The name "Kamathis" covers a large number of more or less skilled labourers from Andhra Pradesh. The Gazetteer of Bombay Presidency (1882, pp. 119-120, Vol. XIII) records "The name is commonly supposed to come from Kām work, because they are good labourers. But as the name is applied to so many castes, it seems to be the name of a district or province, perhaps Komometh to the south east of Haidrabad". According to Enthovan (1922:133) "the term (Kamathi) includes a few scattered immigrant members of Munnurwars, Golevārs, Gullodās, Mungalollās and Saledās, who speak Telugu and came to the presidency some hundred years ago from Hyderabad and Madras".

During the second quarter of eighteenth century Peshwa's rule was at its nadir, and shifted his head quarters to Pune. Many traders, skilled artisans were attracted to the city from different parts of the country, because of the concessions and facilities offered by the Peshwa government. Among the immigrants all sorts of people were included, artisans, traders, masons, priests, soldiers and sepoys. It is said that many of the immigrants were specially invited by the Peshwa to work in his various military departments and for the construction of his city capital. Gadgil (1945:25) noted that "It is remarkable that the more skilled even among ordinary craftsmen of Poona in the later days of Peshwa rule were migrants from other regions".

During the Peshwas rule silk and cotton weaving was at its peak. This attracted many "Kosti" families from the neighbouring states. The first batch of Telugu Momin families migrated to Pune and settled at Ganjpeth during the middle of eighteenth century. Other weaving communities like "Khatris", "Koshtis" from Nagpur and Swakunsalis from Narayan peth of Nizam dominion immigrated during this period and settled at Ganjpeth. In those days, there was a great demand for silk sarees with golden and silver border like "Paithan" and "Pithamber". So during the middle of 18th century itself, Ganjpeth formed the nucleus for handloom industry.

During the later decades of 18th century Peshwas expanded the city capital by constructing huge buildings and temples. To meet this demand many skilled labourers came from different parts of the country. This attracted a large number of labourers from Andhra Pradesh. In addition to construction works, there were ample opportunities for the immigrants to get jobs in various branches of military establishment of the Peshwa. A large number of masons and skilled labourers migrated from Nizam dominion and settled at Shukrawar peth and Vetal. The settlement was named after them — Kamathipura. Peshwa had a special liking for the Kamathis since they were hard working and sincere. Many of them were employed in his military services in order to operate guns and cannons. Moreover they were also employed in his secret services as well as his personal security guards.

Like the artisans and labourers, many pilgrims, especially vedic scholars and priests from all over the country were attracted to the capital city of the Peshwa's. He had constructed temples at Parvathi Hill which was adorned with beautiful shrines. So this attracted many pilgrims from different places. During the month of Shravan many Brahmins and vedic scholars from all over the country used to assemble at Parvathi Hill in order to receive gold and silver as "Dakshinas" from the hands of the Peshwa, after they had been tested by the learned shastris of his court and certified as fit to receive "Dakshina".

As in the case of the Telugu labourers and artisans, the Peshwa had special liking for the Telugu Brahmins. It is said that the Peshwa used to invite the Telugu Brahmins from Nizam dominion in order to perform his rituals and pujas in his court and temple, because they were well versed in chanting the vedic mantras. In return the Peshwa gave them presents as well as money. The Peshwa used to give free food and shelter for the Brahmins who came from outside. In addition to this he offered free land and monetary help to those who wanted to settle in Pune. However, in those days brahmins used to return to their native place when the religious functions were over.

With the decline of the Peshwas regime the influx of immigrants into Pune city also declined. Many of those employed in Peshwa's army and in his court became jobless. Simultaneously the cotton and silk industry also declined. Many of the immigrants who became jobless went back to their native place.

During the pre-colonial era the immigrants were mainly of lower caste workers. Many of the lower caste community workers who came at the time of the Peshwas were employed in his military services and as construction workers and some were weavers. The initial settlements were formed at Shukrawar Peth, Vetal, and Ganj Peth (shown in the Map 2.1). With the decline of the Peshwa's regime many of them became jobless and returned home. They have not formed associations of any sort during their stay at these particular localities. It may be because their numbers were very few and concentration in certain particular localities might have enhanced informal interpersonal relations among themselves. Moreover, migration was male oriented and not with their families. Similarly brahmin priests who migrated during the Peshwas times were not settled permanently even though they were given all sorts of facilities to settle down. Since the migration and settlement was temporary, chances of formation of

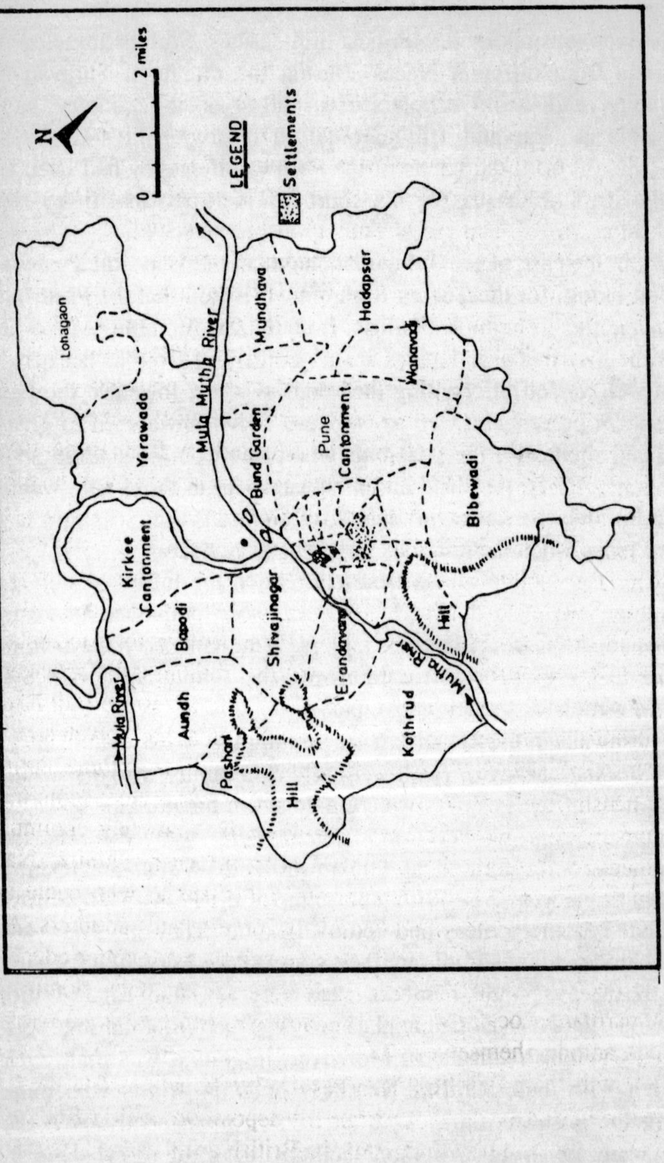

MAP 2.1: Map showing the Settlement areas of the Immigrants during the Pre-colonial period

association were minimal. The immigrants who stayed back formed the nucleus for the migration and settlement during the colonial period.

Colonial Period

The second phase of migration of Telugu speaking people to Pune started during the early stages of British regime in India. During the initial stages of British in India, the Nizam at Hyderabad was on good terms with Lord Wellesley, who was the Governor General of British India. The British and the Nizam used to make treaties so as to help each other at the time of war. According to the treaties of 1792 and 1799 between the Nizam and the British which is known as "*Ceded Districts*", the Nizam agreed to give almost all his troops, cavalry, chivalry to the Britishers against the enemy at the time of war.

In 1802 Yeshwantrao Holkar invaded Pune and drove Baji Rao Peshwa from Peshwaship. In order to restore Baji Rao Peshwa II to the Peshwaship, Colonel Stevenson with a subsidiary from Hyderabad and General Wellesley from Madras with infantry and cavalry marched to Pune in order to fight with Marathas. In the military regiments which came from Madras, as well as that from Hyderabad, many of the south Indians were employed as contractors and labourers. The Gazetteer of Bombay Presidency (1954:158) states that "the first batch of South Indians settled in Poona were the military contractors and labourers under their service, who were engaged for Commissariat arrangements. by Sir Arthur Wellesley in his campaign 1803 to restore Baji Rao II to the Peshwaship, from which Yashwantrao Holkar had driven him".

The first batch of Telugu immigrants who came to Pune along with the British regiment consisted of mainly lower caste communities from the Nizam dominion. They include the following communities: Munnurwars, Mannewar, Gollas, Dhobi, Mochis, Shimpi, Nai and Cobblers. According to the informants the people who came at this period were contractors and Class IV workers, and labourers. Among them members of the Mannurwar community were better educated as compared to the rest of the caste groups, and they dominated in number. They were employed as contractors and held good position in the military.

The final defeat of Baji Rao Peshwa by the British and the capture of Pune took place in 1818. After the deposition of Baji Rao Peshwa, Pune became the headquarters of the British army in the Deccan. After the capture of Pune city many of the Telugu immigrants who came along with the British regiment went back to their native place. To those who stayed back, the British gave free land and financial aid, in order to construct their houses. Since the immigrants were comparatively few in number and most of them were from the same caste and status, they attracted one another to settle in one ecological area. The majority of them settled in one area at Camp and the residential area was named after them i.e. Kamathipura. Recently the name of the settlement area has been changed as Mominpura because of the influx of Mohammadens. Based on the 1822 Census of Peshwa Dafter, Jamav section the total population of Telugu Kamathi migrants in the city of Pune is given in Table 2.1

TABLE 2.1: Population of Kamathis in the city of Pune during 1822

Caste	Families	Adult males	Adult females	Young males	Young females	Total
Kamathi	304	480	626	180	137	1,423

Source: Extracted from "Pune A Socio-economic Survey Part II", 1954, D.R. Gadgil, p. 26.

Earlier settlements of Telugu migrants at the time of the British were mainly in the Cantonment areas of Pune city. Later on, a few of them shifted to Kirkee Cantonment areas. All the Telugu migrants who came along with the British regiment were mainly from Nizamabad and Telangana districts of Nizam dominion. As mentioned above, among the immigrants Munnurwars were in large number and they dominated all the other lower caste migrants in education and economic power. Eminent leaders like Rao Shahib Balkrishan Sayana Motadu and Advocate Polas Rajanna worked for the welfare of the Telugu communities during the middle of 18th century. In order to spread education among the Telugu lower caste communities, as early as 1882, Polas Rajanna Vakil with the help of other prominent leaders formed the "Camp Education Society". In order to give stipend and scholarship to the Telugu students simultaneously they had started "Telugu Education Fund". In 1903 they had also opened "Telugu Library" for the immigrants. Especially the Munnurwars, who were better educated as compared to other migrants, entered into better positions in Pune Municipality. In 1870 Rao Shahib Balkrishna Sayana Motadu became the member of the Cantonment Committee of Pune.

During the 1897-1900, Pune was under severe famine and plague.

This made many of the Telugu immigrants go back to their native place. When the plague and the famine subsided the population of Telugu speaking people in the city of Pune showed substantial reduction in their number.

Since the members of Telugu migrants during the later years of 19th century were comparatively few and there was no proper organization for the management of community activities, to help each other and to organize various religious and cultural activities Telugu speaking people, especially those who had the same status and interests, came together and formed the caste Federation -- "Samastha Telugu Manad Panchayat" in 1913. It is said by the informants that the caste federation was functioning informally even before 1913. But official records are not available. This federation was functioning on lines similar to those of the village caste panchayat, since many of the castes did not have properly organized caste panchayats during this stage. The main intention of this federation was to bring all the Telugu speaking communities under one banner, and to help the members in various ways as, for example at the time of marriage and funerals; to settle any sorts of judicial matters among them; to make them aware of the importance of education, to request members to abstain from drinks and to arrange religious festivals.

In the course of time the already settled immigrants who came during the initial stage of British brought their relatives and friends to the city. Simultaneously this resulted in the multiplication of members in each community. When the old settlements at Camp got saturated, people started moving to other parts of the city and each community formed its own caste panchayat and other welfare associations. At this stage many communities split off from the old caste federation and started strengthening their own caste, by forming various associations. This ultimately resulted in the weakening of the federation. Today this caste federation is on the verge of its extinction.

During the colonial period when the immigrants settled permanently in Pune city, a need arose for Brahmins to perform religious and social ceremonies for the immigrants. In order to meet these demands the first Brahmin namely, Ram Bhat Rajaram Saraswathvaru, with his family (four sons and two daughters) migrated to Pune from the Kushtapuram village of Nizamabad state and settled in old Kamathipura at Camp. Even now most of the religious and ritual ceremonies of the early settlers and their descendants are performed by this family. One of the Saraswathi Brahmins informed us that they follow the traditional method of religious ceremonies for the Telugu speaking people in Pune.

The initial settlements of the Telugu lower caste communities who came with the British regiment during the initial stages are mainly located at Pune and Kirkee Cantonment areas. Later on they shifted to different localities. The areas of settlement of these communities along with the total population according to the enumeration taken by each community is given below. (Settlement areas are shown in the Map 2.2 on the basis of community).

Munnurwars

According to the community enumeration there are 250 Munnurwar families in the city of Pune. They are mainly concentrated in the localities of Rasta Peth, Laskhar, Sholapur Bazaar, Shukrawar Peth, Cyprus and Vaitalwadi. They mainly immigrated from Nizamabad, Nanded and Karimnagar districts of Nizam dominion.

Telugu Dhobis

Two types of endogamous groups have been studied under Telugu Dhobis: they are Telugu Madelwar and Telugu Mallepoolu Gotra. Telugu Madelwars are mainly concentrated in the following areas of Pune city: Sholapur Bazaar, Sadar Bazaar, Modikhana, Pune Camp, Ghorpadi, Kirkee and Cyprus. According to the enumeration of the community the total number of families who came under this group is around 600, whereas the number of families which come under Mallepoolu gotra is comparatively small in number, about 25 families, and they are mainly concentrated in the Camp. Telugu Madelwars migrated from Secunderabad and Hyderabad, whereas the Mallepoolu gotra members came from the Trimalgiri village of Secunderabad. Inter-marriage between these two groups is restricted by their respective panchayats.

Telugu Shimpis

The total number of families of Telugu Shimpis in Pune city is around 700, according to the community enumeration. The initial settlements of Shimpis were mainly at the Camp and Kirkee Cantonment areas. Those Shimpis who are staying at Kirkee and Camp are mainly

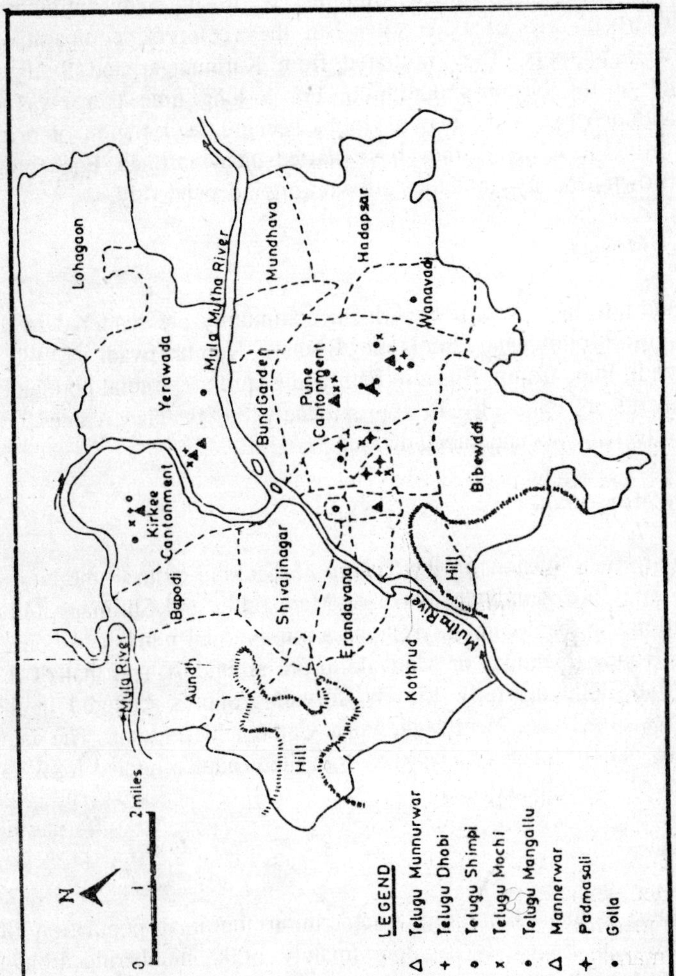

MAP 2.2: Map showing settlement areas of Telugu Immigrant Communities in Pune city and Contonment areas

from Telengana districts of Nizam dominion. Today many of them have moved to the outskirts of the city because of the urban saturation. Another group of Telugu Shimpis is mainly concentrated at Budhwarpeth area of Pune city. But they comprise comparatively recent immigrants. They migrated from Karimnagar and Siddipeth district of the Nizam's dominion. For a long time there was no interaction between these two groups because their region of origin was different. Recently they have started inter-marriage. Each group has its own panchayat and they are working independently.

Telugu Mochis

In Pune city members of the Mochi community are scattered in the areas of Mothikhana, Sholapur Bazaar, Kumbharwadi, Lashkar, Ghorpadi, Pune Camp, Bhavani Peth and Cyprus. The total population of Mochis in Pune city is approximately 3,000. They came from Hyderabad and Secunderabad districts.

Telugu Mangalollu

There are two divisions in the Telugu Mangalollu caste in the city of Pune. They are Konda (Nabhik) or Mangalollu and Shrimangalollu. According to the community enumeration the total number of houses of the Konda (Nabhik), or Mangalollu are around 70 and that of the Shri Mangalollu are only 15. The former group is scattered in the localities of Kirkee, Yerawada, Pune Camp and Laskhar. The later group is mainly located at Kirkee. Both the groups migrated from the villages of Hyderabad district.

Mannewars

According to the community enumeration the total population of Mannewars in Pune city is approximately 1,000, numbering around 250 families. They are mainly settled at Kirkee and Pune Cantonment areas. Today some of them have even moved up to Pimpri and Chinchwed areas of Pune. They migrated from Nizamabad district.

Gollas

Four endogamous groups have been studied under this caste. They are Yeyegolla, Mudutigolla, Eragolla, and domatigolla. Gollas are mainly concentrated in the areas of Pune and Kirkee Cantonment, Nanapeth and Vanavadi. They migrated from Hyderabad and Secunderabad districts. Inter-marriages are restricted among these sub-castes by the respective panchayats.

Padmasalis

After the fall of the Peshwas, the cotton and silk weaving industry was affected very badly in the city. However, it flourished again at the time of the British, during the later years of the 19th century. Migration to and settlement of Padmasalis in Pune started during the later years of the 19th century due to famine and epidemics. They migrated to Pune at various stages. According to Kakadi (1952:115) the migration of Padmasalis during the time of Nizam to the neighbouring states was due to difficulty in finding adequate means of livelihood, due to failure of crops, or due to some other natural calamity. The first Padmasali family, by name Pedda Narayan Jalgi, arrived at Pune from Narayanpeth of Nizam dominion during the later years of 19th century. They left Nizamabad because of natural disasters such as epidemic and famine and walked down to Pune. The Gazetteer of Bombay Presidency states (1886:185-86) "since the 1876-77 famine, about twenty Kāmāthi families have come from Narayan Peth in the Nizām's country and settled at Poona. They own about 100 silks looms and are hardworking and are more successful than either the Musalmāns, Khatris or the local Koshtis". Regarding the handloom industry in Pune, Gadgil extracts the following accounts from the Gazetteer (1945:104); "there were 1,100 to 1,300 looms in Poona during the year 1883-84, the industry was divided into cotton and silk. Cotton weaving was not as thriving as silk weaving. Workers belonged to both the Hindus and Mohamadian communities. Amongst the Hindus 300 looms were worked by Koshti and 150 by the Salis. Except for two families from Madras, the Hindu weavers were said to come from Paithan, Yeola, Sholapur, Indapur, and Narayanpeth in the Nizam territories".

During the Peshwa's time it was the local Koshtis and Mohamadians who dominated the silk and cotton weaving industries in Pune. Padmasalis had a special ability in weaving silk and cotton sarees and gradually they dominated this industry. The initial settlement of Padmasalis who came from Narayanpeth was at Ganjpeth, where already the nucleus of handloom industry was formed during the Peshwa's time. Padmasalis who settled initially, induced their friends , relatives and villagers to emigrate to the city. Further migration and settlement of Padmasalis continued through chain migration.

At this stage another group of Padmasalis from Nizamabad and Karimnagar districts followed the earlier settlers and they settled at Bhavanipeth. The subsequent migration of Padmasalis from Nizamabad and Karimnagar districts increased through chain migration. When the Bhavanipeth area was saturated many of them moved to Nanapeth and Ganjpeth. Today the main concentration of this group is at Bhavanipeth, Nanapeth and Ganjpeth. The migration and settlement of Padmasalis continued till the end of the colonial period. A survey conducted by Gokhale Institute of Politics and Economics in 1936-37 at Ganjpeth, Bhavanipeth, Nanapeth, Vetal, and Ghorpadi revealed that Padmasalis dominated the handloom industry in Pune during the early years of the 20th Century. The Table 2.2 shows this trend.

TABLE 2.2: Classification of Weavers Families by Castes

Caste	Ganj-peth	Bhavani-peth	Nanapeth	Vetal	Ghorpade	total
Padmasali	231	282	88	—	—	601
Swakunsali	67	—	—	20	—	87
Swakunsali Paithan	23	—	—	—	—	23
Momin	46	—	—	24	15	85
Total	367	282	88	44	15	796

Earlier, the handloom industry was in the hands of local Koshtis as well as Telugu Momins. During the early decades of 20th Century it was transferred mainly to the Padmasalis. The above table also shows that the handloom industry is mainly concentrated at Ganjpeth and Bhavanipeth. The influx of Padmasali migrants continued because of the growth of weaving industry as well as beedi industry. The Beedi industry induced the immigrants to move with their families. Even today a good number of women folks are involved in beedi making. During the initial stages many of the Padmasalis were working under the Momin and local Koshtis. Later on they started their own looms. Telugu Padmasalis had a special skill in weaving the "Paithan",

"Pithamber", "Barimal Karaheri" (with golden border), a skill which no other Koshtis had, and these wares were in great demand in those days.

Earlier the Padmasalis got raw materials, such as Yarn and Chemicals, from the Marwadi shops at Bhavani peth on the basis of loans, and finished sarees were sold to them at a reduced price. During the 1940s competition between the handloom and powerloom industry was at its peak. Since the price of powerloom products were less compared to that of the handloom products, the demands for handloom cloths declined. Till the late 1940s many of them carried on their business individually and because of this they found it very difficult to get markets for their products. In order to save the community members from the cruel hands of the Marwardis and to help them to get the raw materials and find markets for their products, the first handloom cooperative society was founded at Ganjpeth on 14th March, 1947. Today the Padmasalis in Pune city have several weaver's cooperative societies, and many of the handlooms have been replaced by powerlooms

Two endogamous groups are found among the Padmasalis in Pune city. Padmasalis who came from Narayanpeth area of Nizamabad district and settled mainly at Ganjpeth are known as Panchmahal Padmasalis. They have their own caste panchayats and other welfare associations. The other group which migrated from Nizamabad and Karimnagar district is mainly settled at Bhavanipeth and Nanapeth. During the early stage of their migration, settlement was on the basis of village and kinship ties. People from different villages clustered in distinct groups at Bhavanipeth. Each group had its own caste panchayat with a "Chowdhary". Later on all the people who came from Nizamabad and Karimnagar district came together and formed a common caste panchayat. In practice even now both the Padmasalis maintain their endogamy and inter-sub-caste marriage is prohibited by the respective panchayats. In the localities where the padmasalis concentrated, especially Bhavani, Ganj and Nana, 75 per cent of the residents are from this community. Because of this proximity they have the highest number of associations than any other Telugu immigrant communities in Pune. Moreover, the immigrants are mainly from one particular village, locality and caste, and this has enabled them to have more informal associations. This contributed positively to the preservation of their social and cultural identity. And this is the only community of those that who migrated during the colonial period which speaks Telugu at home.

In Pune city, Padmasali dominate in numbers all other immigrant communities from Andhra Pradesh. According to community enumeration of 1960, the total population of Padmasalis who came from Nizamabad and Karimnagar district is approximately 20,000, whereas the total population of Panchmahal Padmasalis who came from Narayanpeth area of Mahaboob Nagar district is 2,467, according to the enumeration taken on 15th August, 1981. Among them males above 21 years numbered 644 and children 1,105. Altogether there are 718 houses belonging to Panchmahal Padmasalis.

The next consecutive migration of Telugu speaking people at the time of colonial period started during the First and Second World Wars. By the end of 19th Century the Bombay-Pune Peninsular railway extended up to Madras and the border of Andhra Pradesh. This easy means of transport helped the South Indian people to migrate to Pune during the First and Second World Wars. During this period military establishments were expanded and a few military accounts offices were also opened in Pune city. This attracted many educated Telugu people to avail of these better employment opportunities. Many of the people migrated as a response to advertisement and others were brought by their relatives who had already settled in Pune. During the later decades of the colonial period, it was mainly the educated and upper and middle caste community members who dominated in number. Those who were brought by their relatives who were already settled in Pune settled in the old residential areas. Others scattered wherever accommodation was available. Many of the immigrants settled at Rastha Peth where the South Indian upper and middle caste immigrants had already settled.

During the 1940s the first regional association for the Telugu speaking people was formed by educated and upper and middle caste members, who were scattered all over the city. Even though membership to this association was opened for all Telugu speaking people it was and is managed and dominated by upper and middle caste and educated people. This association helped the immigrants, who were scattered all over the city to come together and participate in various socio-cultural activities arranged by the association.

Post Colonial Period

During the early decades of 20th century there was a decline in weaving industry because of the heavy competition between the handloom and powerloom products. The influx of padmasali weavers into Pune continued till the 1950s. Many people found jobs in powerloom industries which sprang up during the early years of 20th century. Another reason which facilitated the immigration of Padmasalis till the 1950s was the beedi industries which flourished during the early years of 20th century.

Pune city developed as an educational centre during the time of British. With the establishment of the University of Poona in 1948 a new chapter was added in the history of education in Pune. Many people from the south and neighbouring states migrated to Pune in order to acquire higher education.

After the 1950s rapid industrialization brought about ample opportunities for employment for the immigrants in various industrial establishments. Recently three industrial townships Pimpri, Chinchwad and Bhosari have been developed. In addition to this the expansion of defence accounts offices and artillery establishments attracted many of the educated class. Table 2.3 shows the distribution of South Indian population in Pune district from 1911 to 1971.

The distribution of Telugu people in the Pune district shows that among the South Indians Telugu speaking people dominate in number at all stages of migration. One of the reasons may be the geographical proximity. The table shows that there is a tremendous increase of migrants after 1931. The Census of 1951 shows that there is a six fold increase of immigrants over the figure given by the 1931 Census.

The type of migration that is observed at present is mainly individual migration. Many of the migrants came to Pune because of job transfer or direct appointment in Government establishments or private firms. The ethnic settlements which were formed during the pre-colonial and colonial periods got saturated and people started moving to different localities or suburbs of the city wherever accommodation was available. Many of the government employees were provided accommodation in residential quarters near to institution; those who could not get accommodation moved to various parts of the city in search of the same. So during this period, widely scattered types of settlements are found. However, gravitation group settlements are also observed, especially in the outskirts of the city, among immigrants who could not find accommodation in the older settlements.

TABLE 2.3: South Indian Immigrants in Pune District from 1911 to 1971

Language	1911*		1931*		1951*		1961**		1971***	
	Male	Female	Male	Female	Male	Female	Male	Female	Male	Female
Telugu	—	—	2951	2594	17243	15322	28684	21855	31445	28241
Kannada	625	1169	2672	1885	11039	7832	9650	8038	16559	13588
Tamil	—	—	118	1222	11102	8216	14775	11573	16755	13990
Malayalam	—	—	1167	26	1513	1437	7057	3016	10997	5298

* *Gazetteer of Bombay State District* series, 1954, Vol. XX, Part III, Chapter 3, Central Government Press.
** *Census of India 1961*, Vol. X, Maharashtra Part II-C (1), Social and Cultural Tables, Central Government Press.
*** *Census of India 1971*, Maharashtra, Part II-C (1), Social and Cultural Tables, Central Government Press.

Conclusion

Although, migration and settlement of Telugu speaking people to Pune city had begun during the time of Shivaji, no valid documents or reliable data are available to substantiate the pattern of migration and settlement at this period.

During the pre-colonial period migration and settlement was temporary. The immigrants at this period were mainly lower caste community members and migration was group oriented. At this period main settlements were formed at Ganjpeth, Shukrawar peth and Vetal. Since the migration and settlement was temporary, the chances of formation of association were very minimal. Moreover, the number of immigrants was small. Settlement in one particular locality might have enabled them to have informal interpersonal interactions and to satisfy their needs by mutual aid. With the fall of the Peshwa regime many of the settlers became jobless and went back to their native place. Only a few of them remained who could overcome the difficulties of the situation.

The major migration of lower caste people was during the later decades of colonial era. In the beginning of colonial period settlements were mainly in Pune and Kirkee Cantonment areas. During the colonial period the first settlement was formed at Camp by the lower caste immigrants who came with the British regiments. This settlement was formed on the basis of common caste status. Since the number of immigrants during the initial stages was small, all the lower caste members who had the same status fused together and formed a caste federation. This federation acted as adaptive and adjustive mechanism for the immigrants during the initial stages of their settlement. The settled immigrants brought their relatives and friends and caste fellows to the city. When the old settlement got saturated, many of the caste members moved to other parts of the city and settled down on the basis of caste and village. Once the immigrants were well settled in the city, the importance of caste federation decreased and the immigrants split off from the caste federation thereby starting their own welfare associations on the basis of caste. Simultaneously, the functional status of caste federation has become weak.

The main types of migration during the colonial period has been mass migration and chain migration. The Padmasali migration continued till the beginning of post-colonial period. Their migration and settlement was mainly characterised by chain migration and settlement. The Padmasalis are mainly concentrated in three nearby localities i.e. at Bhavanipeth, Ganjpeth and Nanapeth. They settled initially on the basis of village, region-of-origin and sub caste and later, on the basis of caste. During the later stages of colonial period when the immigrants population increased, the associations based on kinship, friendship and family were not sufficient enough to meet their various needs, therefore, associations based on village, sub caste and caste were formed. The settlement formed on the basis of group migration and chain migration helped the Padmasalis to form numerous associations. Today the Padmasalis have the maximum number of associations as compared with other Telugu communities in Pune city.

The settlement formed on the basis of chain migration is prone to form numerous associations. Moreover, the associations formed as a result of chain settlement have shown long term longivity. The associations formed by the Padmasalis and Panchmahal Padmasalis on the basis of chain settlement show these features. In the present study we find that chain settlement, leads initially to the formation of associations at an informal level based on kinship, village and region-of-origin. However, at a later stage, the tendency is to form associations at the sub caste or caste level. Whereas in the case of gravitation settlement, initially, associations are formed at a broader level, based on common culture or caste status. Later on they tend to break down into associations at sub-caste level. Chain settlement facilitates formation of a strong ethnic neighbourhood, whereas the neighbourhood formed on the basis of gravitation group settlement is more prone to dispersal of the ethnic group.

During the later decades of the colonial period, "scattered" pattern of settlement was observed. This type of settlement is more prevalent during the post-colonial period, and it is widely associated with individual migration. The settlements which were formed by migrants during the colonial and pre-colonial period were saturated during the end of the colonial period, which necessitated "scattered" residential pattern. The associations formed as a result of chain settlement and gravitation group settlements were located in the neighbourhood where the immigrants live, while the associations formed as a result of scattered settlement were not always located near the immigrants' residence.

Despite scattered residence, immigrants kept contact with their old settlements through participation in associations which have already been formed there. They have also formed new associations in order to meet their socio-cultural needs. This helped to perpetuate ethnic identity despite ethnic segregation.

3

A TYPOLOGY OF CASTE PANCHAYATS

This chapter deals with the extent to which the traditional institutions, such as caste panchayats, are preserved in the urban setting despite the ongoing process of industrialization and urbanization. Twenty caste panchayats of the Telugu lower caste immigrant communities were analysed on the basis of structural and functional adaptations undergone by them during various stages of their development. A taxonomy of caste panchayats has also been attempted in this chapter. The location of caste panchayats is shown in Map 3.1.

Indian society is stratified mainly on the basis of caste. Matters concerning the internal and external affairs of caste are regulated by caste panchayats or councils. Generally caste panchayats are more prevalent among the lower and middle caste groups and are very weak among Brahmins. Hutton (1963:61) noted that "the lower the caste in the social scale, the stronger its combination and the more efficient its organization".

Several studies are available on the role of caste panchayats in the Indian villages (see M.N. Srinivas, 1954, 1969; Majamdar, 1958; Mayer, 1960; Pradhan, 1966). Various definitions on caste panchayats based on the structural and functional characteristics are also available. Majamdar (1958) described caste council as a judicial system; and Mayer (1960) "as an assembly for meeting for consultation or advice". A review of literature on caste panchayats in the village situation has shown the following characteristics:

(i) the caste council or panchayat acts only for a limited area;
(ii) the officials who perform its executive and judicial functions may be appointed ad-hoc or for a particular period or hereditary;
(iii) it acts as a judicial system; and
(iv) it is the main basis by which endogamy of the caste is retained.

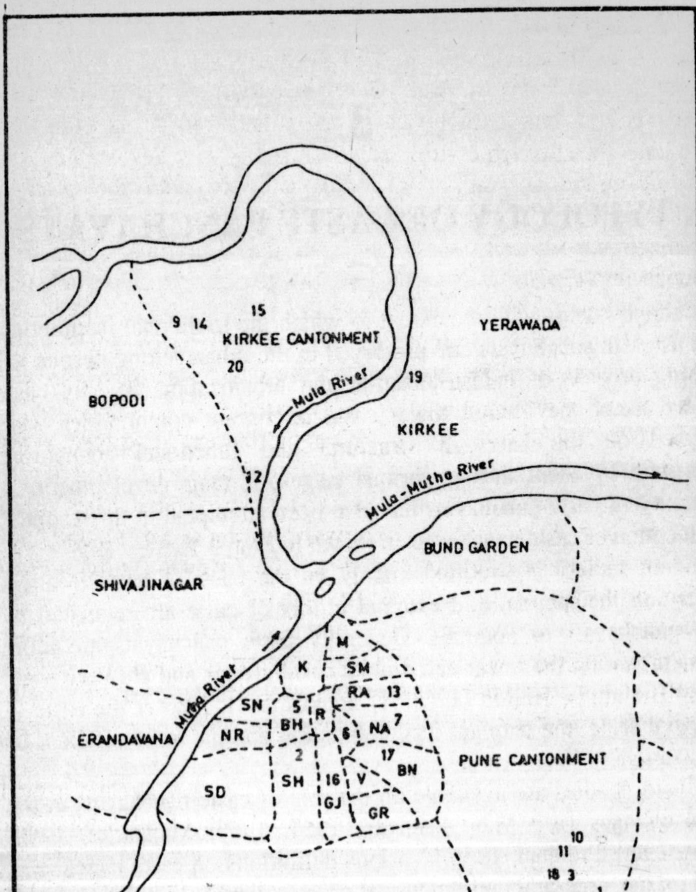

MAP 3.1: Map showing locations of Caste Panchayats

Notes:

1. Telugu Hindu Mala Union, Camp.
2. Sukrawarpeth Munnurwar Jynatha Ganga, Shukrawarpeth.
3. Munnurwar Jynatha Ganga, Bhimpura.
4. Modati Golla Samaj, Sholapur Bazaar.
5. Shankardas Mayya Maru, Budhwarpeth.
6. Domati Golla Samaj, Sholapur Bazaar.
7. Yadav Golla Samaj, Nanapeth.
8. Mudut Golla Samaj, Sholapur Bazaar.
9. Telugu Konda (Nabhik) Samaj, Kirkee.
10. Telugu Madelwar Samaj, Lashkar.
11. Shankardas Mayya Bhakth Telugu Shimpi Samaj, Camp.
12. Telugu Mannewar Samaj, Kirkee.
13. Munnurwar Jynatha Ganga, Rasthapeth
14. Telugu Mochi Samaj, Kirkee.
15. Telugu Madelwar Samaj, Kirkee.
16. Padmasali Panch Committee Ganjpeth.
17. Padmasali Panch Committee Bhavanipeth.
18. Mochi Samaj, Lashkar.
19. Kirkee Munnurwar Jynatha Ganga, Kirkee.
20. Telugu Shimpi Samaj, Dargigalli.

The study of caste panchayats in the urban setting shows, that each caste has its own panchayat at the sub-caste level and membership is acquired by birth or ascribed. All the twenty caste panchayats under study showed that initially all of them had similar structural and functional features and during various stages of their development they had undergone adaptations in order to cope with the changing conditions. All of them have been analysed at three levels: organization, democratization and activity. They also have been grouped into types, mainly stressing the authority structure as well as their functions.

The degree of adaptations undergone by each panchayat varies. Based on the degree of adaptations, the twenty caste panchayats were classified into three types. They are: (1) Fused, (2) Transitional and (3) Differentiated.[1] Out of the twenty, six represent the fused type, twelve fall into the transitional type and the remaining two represent differentiated type. Fused panchayats are those which have similar structural and functional characteristics to those of village caste panchayat, they are least adapted to the changing urban scene. Transitional panchayats are in the stage of transition where the traditional characteristics of caste panchayat and modern organizational features co-exist. The last type, differentiated, is better adapted to the changing urban conditions and most of the traditional characteristics are atrophied and modern organizational characteristics projected outside.

In order to group the panchayats into type, first an attempt is made to compare the twenty caste panchayats in the urban setting with village caste panchayats, taking the latter as an ideal type. For comparison authority structure and their major functions such as regulation of marriage and as judicial systems, are taken into consideration. They have been further analysed at the levels, organization, activity, and democratization. Finally, the historical development of each type of panchayat has been attempted showing examples from each type.

Table 3.1 shows the classification of caste panchayats based on the comparison with the village caste panchayat. For comparison, the authority structure of the village caste panchayat and its major functions are examined. The table clearly shows that the characteristics of fused panchayats and the village caste panchayats are almost the same. Variation is not considerable between them. Fused panchayats have retained almost all the characteristics of the village caste panchayat. In the transitional type we see that they have undergone considerable adaptations while retaining most of the characteristics of the village caste panchayat. All the panchayats have undergone structural and functional adaptation. The authority structure, in most of the cases show a combination of traditional and democratic types of authority. By retaining all major functions that are seen in the village context, most of the panchayats have taken up religious, educational and social welfare activities. The third type of panchayats have undergone considerable structural and functional adaptation. Most of the characteristics of the traditional caste panchayats have been atrophied and they have incorporated some of the modern organizational features. The first and the third type do not show much variation within the group. However, in the second type there is considerable variations within the group itself. This is because they are in a stage of transition. Intra-group variation is not significant, whereas the inter-group variation is highly significant.

Table 3.2 shows the classification of caste panchayats based on levels of organization, activity, and democratization. If we move from the fused type to the differentiated type, we may see that the major variations are recorded on account of registration, and democratization. In the transitional type majority of the panchayats have a traditional-democratic type of procedure for the selection of office bearers. However, a few panchayats among them have already adapted democratic line of selection of the office bearers, although in practice they do not follow the democratic principles on other issues. There is some variation within the group itself, but these variations are very negligible. But the inter-group variation is highly significant.

TYPE I : FUSED

Authority Structure

In the first type, the authority structure is similar to that of village caste panchayat . In most of the cases, the president's[2] post is filled hereditarily. If this post is not inherited then an elderly or respected person from the community assumed this position. All the office bearers posts are selected or nominated by an elderly person in the community. In certain cases the president is responsible for managing the panchayat activities. Still in others, the president, with the help of committee members, manages the panchayat activities.

TABLE 3.1: Comparison of Urban Caste Panchayat with that of village Caste Panchayat.

Type	Urban Caste Panchayat									Village Caste Panchayat								
	Authority Structure			Rules of endogamy		Judicial function		Sanction of marriage	Other function	Authority structure			Rules of endogamy		Judicial function		Sanction marriage	Other function
1	1	2	3	4	5	6	7	8	9	1	2	3	4	5	6	7	8	9
TYPE I : FUSED																		
1. Telugu Hindu Mala Union, Camp	+	—	—	+	—	+	—	+	—	+	—	—	+	—	+	—	+	—
2. Shukrawarpeth Munnurwar Jynatha Ganga	+	—	—	+	—	+	—	+	—	+	—	—	+	—	+	—	+	—
3. Munnurwar Jynatha Ganga, Bhimpura	+	—	—	+	—	+	—	+	—	+	—	—	+	—	+	—	+	—
4. Modati Golla Samaj, Sholapur Bazaar	+	—	—	+	—	+	—	+	—	+	—	—	+	—	+	—	+	—
5. Shankardas Mayya Maru, Budhwar Peth	+	—	—	+	—	+	—	+	—	+	—	—	+	—	+	—	+	—
6. Domati Golla Samaj, Sholapur Bazaar.	+	—	—	+	—	+	—	+	—	+	—	—	+	—	+	—	+	—

Contd.

TABLE 3.1 *(Contd.)*

1	1	2	3	4	5	6	7	8	9	1	2	3	4	5	6	7	8	9
TYPE II : TRANSITIONAL																		
1. Yadav Golla Samaj, Nanapeth.	—	+	—	+	—	+	—	+	+	+	—	—	+	+	+	—	+	—
2. Samastha Jynatha Ganga Mudut Gollollu Yadav Gauli Samaj, Sholapur Bazaar.	—	+	—	+	—	+	—	+	+	+	—	—	+	—	+	—	+	—
3. Telugu Konda (Nabhik) Samaj, Kirkee.	—	+	—	+	—	+	—	+	—	+	—	—	+	—	+	—	+	—
4. Telugu Madelwar Samaj, Lashkar.	—	+	+	+	—	+	—	+	+	+	—	—	+	—	+	—	+	—
5. Shankardas Mayya Bhakth Telugu Shimpi Samaj, Camp.	—	+	—	+	—	+	—	+	+	+	—	—	+	—	+	—	+	—
6. Telugu Mannewar Samaj, Kirkee.	—	+	—	+	—	+	—	+	+	+	—	—	+	—	+	—	+	—
7. Munnurwar Jynatha Ganga, Rasthapeth.	—	+	+	+	—	+	—	+	+	+	—	—	+	—	+	—	+	—
8. Telugu Mochi Samaj, Kirkee.	—	+	—	+	—	+	—	+	+	+	—	—	+	—	+	—	+	—
9. Telugu Madelwar Samaj, Kirkee.	—	—	+	+	—	+	—	+	+	+	—	—	+	—	+	—	+	—
10. Padmasali Panch Committee Ganjpeth.	—	—	—	+	—	+	—	+	+	+	—	—	+	—	+	—	+	—
11. Padmasali Panch Committee Bhavanipeth.	—	—	—	+	—	+	—	+	+	+	—	—	+	—	+	—	+	—
12. Mochi Samaj, Lashkar.	—	—	+	+	—	+	—	+	+	+	—	—	+	—	+	—	+	—

TABLE 3.1 (*Contd.*)

1	1	2	3	4	5	6	7	8	9	1	2	3	4	5	6	7	8	9
TYPE III : DIFFERENTIATED																		
1. Kirkee Munnurwar Jynatha Ganga, Trust	—	—	+	—	+	—	+	+	+	+	—	—	+	—	+	—	+	—
2. Telugu Shimpi Samaj, Dargigalli	—	—	+	—	+	—	+	+	+	+	—	—	+	—	+	—	+	—

(1) Hereditary or Nomination
(2) Traditional Democratic
(3) Democratic
(4) Strict
(5) Weak
(6) Strict
(7) Weak
(8) Sanctioning of marriage
(9) Functions other than sanction of marriage and judicial function.

+ = shows presence of the trait
— = shows absence of the trait.

TABLE 3.2: Classification of Caste Panchayats based on level of organization, level of activity and level of democratisation

Type	Level of Organisation							Level of Activity					Level of Democratisation							
	1	2	3	4	5	6	7	8	9	10	11	12	13	14a	14b	14c	15	16	17	18
TYPE I : FUSED																				
1. Telugu Hindu Mala Union, Camp	+	—	+	+	—	—	—	+	—	—	+	—	+	—	+	—	—	—	—	—
2. Shukrawarpeth Munnurwar Jynatha Ganga	+	—	+	—	—	—	+	+	—	+	—	—	+	—	—	+	—	—	—	—
3. Munnurwar Jynatha Ganga, Bhimpura	+	+	+	+	—	—	+	+	+	+	—	+	+	—	+	+	—	—	—	+
4. Modati Golla Samaj, Sholapur Bazaar	+	—	+	+	—	—	+	+	—	+	+	—	+	—	+	—	—	—	—	+
5. Shankardas Mayya Maru, Bhavani Peth	+	+	+	+	—	—	+	+	—	+	+	—	+	—	+	+	—	—	—	—
6. Domati Golla Samaj, Sholapur Bazaar.	+	+	+	+	—	—	+	+	—	+	+	—	+	—	+	+	—	—	—	+

(Contd.)

TABLE 3.2 (*Contd.*)

	1	2	3	4	5	6	7	8	9	10	11	12	13	14a	14b	14c	15	16	17	18
TYPE II : TRANSITIONAL																				
1. Yadav Golla Samaj, Nanapeth.	+	+	+	—	—	—	+	+	+	+	+	—	+	+	+	—	+	—	—	—
2. Samastha Jynatha Ganga Mudut Gollollu Yadav Gauli Samaj, Sholapur Bazaar.	+	+	+	+	—	—	+	+	+	+	+	—	+	+	+	—	+	—	+	+
3. Telugu Konda (Nabhik) Samaj, Kirkee.	+	+	+	+	+	+	+	+	+	+	+	—	+	+	+	—	+	—	—	+
4. Telugu Madelwar Samaj, Lashkar.	+	+	+	+	+	+	+	+	+	+	+	+	+	+	—	—	+	—	—	+
5. Shankardas Mayya Bhaktha Telugu Shimpi Samaj, Camp.	+	+	+	+	+	+	+	+	+	+	+	+	+	+	—	—	+	—	+	+
6. Telugu Mannewar Samaj, Kirkee.	+	+	+	+	+	+	+	+	+	+	+	—	+	+	+	—	+	—	+	+
7. Munnurwar Jynatha Ganga, Rasthapeth.	+	+	+	+	+	+	+	+	+	+	+	+	+	+	—	—	+	—	+	+
8. Telugu Mochi Samaj, Kirkee.	+	+	+	+	+	+	+	+	+	+	+	+	+	+	+	—	+	—	+	+
9. Telugu Madelwar Samaj, Kirkee.	+	+	+	+	+	+	+	+	+	+	+	+	+	+	+	—	+	—	+	—
10. Padmasali Panch Committee Ganjpeth.	+	+	+	+	+	+	+	+	+	+	—	+	+	+	—	+	+	—	+	+
11. Padmasali Panch Committee Bhavanipeth.	+	+	+	+	+	+	+	+	+	+	+	+	+	+	+	+	+	—	+	+
12. Mochi Samaj, Lashkar.	+	+	+	+	+	+	+	+	+	+	+	+	+	+	—	—	+	—	+	+

(*Contd.*)

TABLE 3.2 *(Contd.)*

	1	2	3	4	5	6	7	8	9	10	11	12	13	14a	14b	14c	15	16	17	18
TYPE III : DIFFERENTIATED																				
1. Kirkee Munnurwar Jynatha Ganga, Trust	+	+	+	+	+	+	+	+	+	+	+	—	+	+	—	—	+	+	+	+
2. Telugu Shimpi Samaj, Dargigalli	+	+	+	+	+	+	+	+	+	+	+	+	+	+	—	—	+	+	+	+

1. Defined decision-making
2. Specified meeting
3. Specified organisational activity
4. Defined activities for office bearers
5. Written rules and regulations
6. Registration.
7. Record keeping
8. Defined criteria for membership
9. General Body meeting
10. Committee meeting
11. Collection of membership fee
12. Presence of common property
13. Presence of common fund

14a. Selection of office bearers by election
14b. Nomination
14c. Hereditary

15. Participation of members in election
16. Regular election
17. General membership participation in decision-making
18. Division of labour among office bearers.

\+ = Shows presence of the trait.
— = Shows absence of the trait.

Regulation of Marriage

Marriage is sanctioned by the president or "Chowdhary" of the respective panchayat. Payment of marriage cess for bride varies from Rs. 5 to Rs. 70, and for groom Rs. 10 to Rs. 70. Rules of endogamy are very strict. If any member goes against the panchayat rules regarding marriage or contracts an inter caste marriage, the member as well as his family do not call for the functions arranged by the panchayat. In some cases the accused can come back as a full–fledged member after paying certain amount as fine.

Judicial Function

Almost all sorts of judicial matters among the members are settled within the panchayat. In some cases the president himself hears the matter and suggests the final decisions. In others the president, in consultation with the committee members, takes the final decision in judicial matters. The 'Chowdhary', or president, of the respective panchayats takes special care that all the matters are settled in the panchayat itself. Usually he never allows the members to go to court to settle their judicial problems.

Level of Organization

Defined Decision-Making

In all these panchayats the decision-making processes are well defined. In two panchayats the 'Chowdhary' has the authority to take any final decision on organizational matters. In the remaining panchayats, the executive committee members with the help of the president finalize the decision.

Defined Meetings

Only the committee meetings are clearly defined. Actually the meetings are not fixed. Wherever, there is some sort of function, or depending upon the need of the panchayat, committee meetings are called. No other type of meeting is found in this type of panchayat.

Specified Organizational Activity

A key function of this type of panchayat is to sanction or attest to the marriage of members and to help them to arrange their marriages and funerals. In addition to this, all the panchayats take keen interest in settling the judicial matters among the members. No other types of functions are undertaken by them.

Registration and Written Rules and Regulation

All the panchayats are unregistered and do not have any written rules and regulations.

Record Keeping

All of them except one keep the important documents regarding the panchayat activities. Since none of them have an office of their own, all documents are kept with the president.

Defined Criteria for Membership

Each panchayat is working at the sub–caste level; membership in each caste panchayat is by birth into the caste and is ascribed.

Level of Activity

General Body Meeting

Among the six panchayats which come under this category, only one panchayat conducts general meetings once in a year. The rest of the panchayats have not arranged any general meeting so far.

Committee Meetings

Committee meetings are not fixed there is a degree of variation in the number of committee meetings that these panchayats conduct. Telugu Hindu Mala Union conduct only one or two committee meetings per year. In all the panchayats the number of committee meetings may increase or decrease depending upon the number of functions arranged by the panchayats. In all the panchayats committee meetings are held in the presidents house, usually in the night when the committee members are free from their work.

Collection of Membership Fee

As a rule all the panchayats collect a monthly subscription fee. But there is a variation in the rate. Among them, two panchayats have stopped collecting membership fee. The Telugu Hindu Mala Union collect the monthly subscription at a rate of Re.1 from each head of the household. It is collected by the brother-in-law of the president. Domatigolla Samaj and Modatigolla Samaj panchayats collect a membership fee of Re.0.50 pei month. Shankaradas Mayyamaru panchayat at Budhwar Peth has a rate of Rs.2 per month.

Exercise of Common Property

Except for one, the panchayats do not have any common property. Only the Munnurwarlu Jynatha Ganga at Bhimpura owns a building, which is used for arranging marriage of the members. No panchayat has its own temple.

Exercise of Common Fund

The main source of income of the panchayat is from membership fee and the "Katnam" that they get at the time of marriage. The income of these panchayats varies from Rs.50 to Rs.150 per month. Presidents of two panchayats informed us that their panchayats do not have any balance; whatever money they get is spent for the maintenance of the panchayat.

Level of Democratization

Selection of Office Bearers

Selection of office bearers is either hereditary or by nomination. Of the six panchayats, the presidents' post is inherited in two. In the remaining panchayats it is by selection or nomination by an elderly person in the community. All the office bearers posts are meant for elderly persons in the community. Democratization is not at all practiced in this panchayat.

Participation of Members in Election

Members are not involved in selecting the office bearers. Influential or elderly persons from the community are nominated or selected for the office bearers' posts.

Regular Election

There is no fixed time for election or nomination of the office bearers. So far not a single panchayat in this type has conducted an election in order to select the office bearers.

General Participation in Decision-Making

Members are not involved in decision-making processes. In certain cases the decision on the organizational matters is taken by the president, in others the president consults the office bearers on this matter.

Division of Labour among the Office Bearers

A democratic type of official body is not at all found in these panchayats. The number of managing committee members is small. Most of the official duties are undertaken by the president, or he shares the official duties with the executive committee members.

In order to show the characteristics of fused panchayat, two cases have been presented. Both the panchayats have been in existence for quite a long time, and the structural and functional adaptations undergone by them are very minimal. There is not much change or adaptation observed in their authority structure or their major functions. Even today these two panchayats have retained almost all the characteristics of the village caste panchayat.

Example I

Telugu Munnurwar Jynatha Ganga: Bhimpura

Until 1955 the Munnurwars staying at Camp had two panchayats. One was located at Lashkar and the other was at Sholapur bazaar. Until then both panchayats worked independently, and were managed by the

'Chowdharys'. In 1955 Lashkar and Sholapur bazaar panchayats fused into one, known as Telugu Munnurwar Jynatha Ganga, Bhimpura. Today under this panchayat 75 members have registered their names. There has been no remarkable change observed in this panchayat from its inception to the present. Even after its fusion, no change in its structure or function was observed.

The official body consists of the president, the vice–president and nine committee members. Even today the presidents post is the monopoly of one family. Over the last few decades the president's post has followed in the same family. An elderly or respected person from the community is nominated for the vice–presidents post. This panchayat is fully managed by elderly persons in the community.

Today the main function of this panchayat is to sanction the marriage of its members and act as a judicial system. No other function is undertaken by this panchayat. The degree of adaptation undergone by this panchayat in its structure and function is very marginal.

Example II

Telugu Hindu Mala Union

This panchayat was not properly organized till 1970, and it was managed by hereditary "Chowdharys". It was reformed in 1970 with the intention of bringing their community members together, to help one another during occasions such as marriages and funerals. This panchayat is mainly managed by one family. The official body consists of one president. This post has continued in the same family for decades. The "Chowdhary" is a respected person from the community. He has the right to take decision on any matter relating to the community.

This panchayat is not registered and does not have written rules and regulations. Meetings are not fixed in this panchayat. One or two meetings every year used to be arranged. So far they have not conducted any general body meeting. The number of meetings depend on the need of the community. If there is any meeting or function, the 'Chowdhary' informs the senior members through one of his relatives.

The main function of this panchayat is to sanction and attest to the marriage of the members, and to act as a judicial system. Rules of endogamy are very strict. If any member goes against the rule of panchayat, especially in the case of marriage, the accused and his family are usually excommunicated. Problems such as disputes, property rights, marriage adjustment, and divorce are settled within the panchayat by the "Chowdhary" himself or with the help of senior persons in the community. The panchayat makes sure that all judicial matters concerning the members are settled within the panchayat itself.

TYPE II : TRANSITIONAL

Authority Structure

Here the democratic authority is superimposed upon the traditional authority. However, the traditional types of authority dominates. In the majority of these panchayats the office bearers' posts are reserved for elderly persons in the community. In a few cases, only the posts of the presidents and the vice–presidents are reserved for elderly and respected persons in the community, although for the remaining posts there are no special criteria. In most cases these posts are filled by younger persons. In almost all the panchayats the majority of the committee members posts are filled by younger persons. The interesting characteristic is that the hereditary and elected managing committee co-exist. Even though the authority structure is shared by elderly persons as well as younger members, the total management of the panchayat is in the hands of older members. All the panchayats except two which come under this category have written rules and regulations. Those panchayats which have written rules and regulations do not strictly follow them in actual behavioural pattern. Even while electing or selecting the office bearers the rules and regulations as written in the constitution are not followed strictly.

Regulations of Marriage

In this type also the rules of endogamy are very strict. If any member breaks the rules of endogamy the accused and his family are excommunicated from the panchayat. They are not called for any functions arranged by the panchayat. Usually the accused can come back as a full-fledged member after paying certain amount as fine. Here also marriage is sanctioned by the president. Marriage cess for brides varies from Rs.2.50 to Rs.20, and for groom from Rs.10 to Rs.30.

Judicial Function

Most of the panchayats of this category have well-organised "Nyaya Committee" to settle the judicial matters. In almost all cases, "Nyaya Committee" is formed by president and a few representative of the committee members. In other cases, where it is absent, when members approach the panchayat to hear the legal matters. "Nyaya Committee" is temporarily formed by the president with the help of office bearers. In most of the panchayats of this type office bearers make sure that all the legal matters regarding the members are settled within the panchayat itself. If anyone goes against the decision of the "Nyaya Committee" a certain amount of money is charged as fine.

Level of Organization

Defined Decision-Making

In all the panchayats the process of decision-making is defined. Members are also involved in decision-making process to a certain extent.

Specified Meetings

Meetings are specified and are followed. Almost all the panchayats arrange two or three committee meetings per month. In some panchayats, members are also allowed to .attend the committee meetings. In the constitution of all the panchayats, the holding of general body meetings is specified.

Specified Organizational Activity

Activities of each panchayat are specified. In addition to the major functions, such as sanction and attestation of marriage and as a judicial system, they have also undertaken educational, religious and other social welfare activities.

Registration and Written Rules and Regulation

Except for two of the 12 panchayats, all are registered and have written or printed rules and regulations. But in actual practice, not a single panchayat follows them strictly.

Record Keeping

Among the panchayats, Padmasali Panch Committee at Bhavanipeth have a partitioned room as the office. The rest of the panchayats do not have their own office. Except in the case, the records and documents of the panchayats are kept with the presidents of the respective panchayats or with an elderly person in the community.

Defined Criteria for Membership

In all the panchayats membership is given at the sub-caste level. Each caste has got its own panchayat at sub-caste level. The criteria of membership are clearly defined. Membership is ascribed and by birth into the caste. According to the president of Padmasali Panch Committee at Bhavanipeth, membership is open for all the members who come under the sub-category of Padmasali caste. But in practice not a single member of panchamahal Padmasali has taken membership in this panchayat.

Level of Activity

General Body Meeting

General Body Meetings are conducted by all the panchayats. The number of general body meetings varies in each panchayat. Padmasali Panch Committee at Bhavanipeth and Telugu Madelwar panchayat at Lashkar arrange four general body meetings every year. And in the remaining panchayats, general body meetings are conducted once in a year. Participation of members in the general body meeting also varies from panchayat to panchayat. In most of the panchayats 50 to 60 per cent of the members used to attend the general body meeting. In the remaining panchayats the number of participating members is low.

Committee Meetings

Committee meetings are held in all the panchayats. In three panchayats the date of committee meeting is fixed monthly. In most of the panchayats the president sends a circular via a messenger, informing the date, place and time of the committee meetings. If the messenger is absent, then the president himself takes charge of informing the executive committee members regarding the meeting. The number of committee meetings also varies from panchayat to panchayat. The number of committee meetings per month ranges from one to four. In each panchayat, committee meetings are arranged at night when, the executive committee members are free from their work. Committee meetings are held in the temple premises or in the house of office bearers, especially that of the president.

Collection of Membership Fee

Of the 12 panchayats all the panchayats collect the monthly subscription fee except the Padmasali Panch Committee at Ganjpeth. The president of Padmasali Panch Committee at Ganjpeth informed us that from 1953 to 1954 they were collecting membership fee at a rate of Re.1.25 per month. Today because the panchayat has enough income to meet the expenses of the community they stopped collecting fees. Out of 20,000 members of Padmasali Punch Committee at Bhavanipeth only 300 members regularly pay the membership fee at a rate of Re.0.50 per month. Mannewar Panchayat at Kirkee have two types of membership; life membership and ordinary membership. Life membership fee is Rs.150. The ordinary membership fee Re.1 per month. In others membership fee varies from Re.0.50 to Rs.2 per month.

In all the panchayats certain procedures are involved in admitting new members. For new migrants who came from outside Pune a long procedure is involved, to acquire membership in Telugu Madelwar panchayat at Kirkee and Lashkar. First of all the migrant has to submit a written application to the president. If the new member does not have a relative of his own to introduce him, then the president writes back to the president of the panchayat of his place of origin asking for information about the new immigrant. Once the president makes sure that the person belongs to their community then the matter is presented in the general body meeting, and with the consent of the members he may be admitted as a member in the panchayat. Telugu Madelwar Panchayat at Kirkee collects Rs.11 from the new member as admission fee in addition to the regular membership fee.

For Telugu Madelwar Panchayat at Lashkar, the entrance fee is not fixed. The new member can pay the amount according to his ability.

This panchayat collect a minimum amount of Rs. 27 from the new migrant in order to acquire membership in the panchayat. This amount covers admission fee of Re. 1.25, Rs. 6 as one year monthly subscription, Rs. 2.50 as "Samaj Sitting" fee, Rs. 11 as temple donation, and the rest Rs. 6.25 as a donation for the Samaj. The remaining panchayats also charge an entrance fee for the new members.

Exercise of Common Property

Of the 12 panchayats which come under this category, eight have common property such as temples, *dharmashalas*, *mangal karyalaya*, or buildings. The remaining four panchayats do not have any common property.

Exercise of Common Fund

The main source of income of all these panchayats is from membership fees, engagement and marriage cess. Moreover, some panchayats get money from buildings and cooking utensils that they give on rental basis. Padmasali Panch Committee at Bhavanipeth, has a common property worth Rs.10 lakhs. Monthly income of this panchayat goes from Rs.2,500 to Rs.3,000. The next highest income in collected by Padmasali Panch Committee at Ganjpeth, which is around Rs.1,000 to Rs.1,500 per month. The rest of the panchayats have their monthly income between Rs.100 to Rs.400.

Level of Democratization

Initial Selection of Office Bearers

The main characteristics of this panchayat is that the democratized system of selection of office bearers has been superimposed upon the traditionally followed hereditary system. But the traditionally followed hereditary method dominates. In almost all the panchayats all sort of high official posts are reserved for elderly persons in the community. In a few cases all the office bearers posts are meant for elderly and respected persons in the community. In none of the panchayats is a real election conducted, rather, it is a sort of selection or nomination to select the office bearers. In almost all the panchayats members of the younger generations are selected as committee members. Even though of 12 panchayats 10 are registered and have written rules and regulations, in actual practice they do not follow them. This is the case even for electing the office bearers.

Participation of Members in Election

Office bearers are selected in the general body meeting. Members are also involved in selecting the office bearers. No panchayat had ballot voting. Most of the candidates selected are unopposed.

Regular Election

No panchayat strictly follows the rules and regulation in holding regular election or selection in time. This is the case with selection or election of trustee's as well.

General Participation in Decision-Making

Members are involved in decision-making processes. In most of the panchayats decisions on policy oriented matters are taken by the executive managing committee members. The decision other than policy matters are taken with the help of members. In two panchayats all sorts of decisions are taken with the help of members.

Division of Labour among the Office Bearers

Division of labour for the office bearers in all the panchayats is defined. All panchayats as well have an organized office body. With mutual agreement among the office bearers, they can transfer their work. The president of Telugu Madelwar Samaj at Kirkee and Yadav Golla Samaj at Nanapeth is in name only. In both, the duties of the president are undertaken by the Secretary of the respective panchayats.

Two cases are presented here to show the changes or adaptations undergone by the transitional type during various stages of their development. Analysis of authority structure of both the panchayats showed that in the beginning authority structure was similar in both cases. In the case of Padmasali Panch Committee the elected office bearers and the hereditarily followed "Chowdhary" System co-exist. In the case of Telugu Madelwar Panchayat, only the presidents post is reserved for the elderly persons in the community, and he is president in name only. Almost all of his duties are done by other office bearers. The rest of the office bearers are elected in the general body meeting. Both of them have undergone considerable functional adaptation, retaining traditional social functions as such as well as undertaking religious, educational and cultural activities.

Example I

Padmasali Panch Committee: Bhavanipeth

During the early stages of migration of Padmasalis the settlement pattern was mainly on the basis of kinship and village. People from particular villages came together and settled in distinct groups. During 1915, there were nine distinct groups, and each of these groups was known as "Phali" or "tat". Each "phali" constitutes a separate sub-group. For each "phali" there was one "Peddamanshi" who was responsible for managing the panchayat activities. The post of "Peddamanshi" was hereditary. The main function of the "Peddamanshi" was to regulate and control the behaviour of its members and sanction the marriage. If a member did not follow the rules and regulations of the panchayat, "Peddamanshi" had the authority to excommunicate or out-caste the member from the Samaj (Ashanna, 1971). "Peddamanshi's" consent was necessary for arranging the marriage of members. In those days as a marriage cess the groom and the bride had to pay an amount of Rs. 44 each. However, when Prof. D.R. Gadgil (1954) undertook his survey in 1952, marriage cess was reduced to Rs. 9. In those days "Peddamanshi" spent the panchayat income for arranging parties or for drinks. In order to save the community income for welfare and to bring all the scattered members under one banner, Shri Shankar Rao Andhe called a meeting in 1935. In that meeting they discussed the disorganization of their community and requested the "Peddamanshis" to use the income for constructive and creative purposes. All the nine "tat" leaders were present in that meeting. In the same year they formed the Padmasali Panch Committee bringing all the "tat" members under one banner, with 25 selected executive members. The Panch was selected from the following families, i.e. Gangi, Adep, Bhandari, Saka and Uplanchi. The "tat" leaders and Panch Possess social power. All sorts of disputes, marriage problems and quarrels were settled within the panchayat itself. The decisions on any matter taken by the "tat" leaders and panch committee members were final. The panch committee members were authorized to control the activities of the community. During 1930-35, the total population of Padmasalis in Pune was approximately 5,000 to 6,000. In 1948 a trust of five members were selected and it was registered as Padmasali Panch Committee.

Present Organizational Structure

The present organizational set up of the Panch committee is partly traditional and partly democratic. The panch committee consists of one selected "Sarpanch" who is the supreme authority in the panchayat. An elderly person who worked for the community is always considered for this post. In addition to him there are executive committee members and "Peddamanshis". The office bearers consist of the president, the vice-president, secretary, joint secretary, treasurer and auditor. Below them there are 33 committee members. The committee members are further divided into sub-committee like "Devasthan Committee", "Utsav Committee", "Barthan Committee" and "Nyaya Committee". Recently most of the committee member's post are filled by members of the younger generation. All the office bearer's posts are elected in the general body meeting.

Peddamanshis

Earlier this panchayat was managed by "Peddamanshis". There were nine "Peddamanshis", six for Bhavanipeth, two for Nanapeth, and one for Ganjpeth. Today the number of "Peddamanshis" has been reduced to five. Out of them only three are doing their duty properly. The rest of the families are not interested in following the same post. Even today the posts of "Peddamanshis" are hereditary. Although the importance of "Peddamanshis" has been reduced. Still they have a role to play in the organizational activities of the community. They take active part in marriage functions and in settling judicial problems among the members. Out of the five "Peddamanshis" two are uneducated and the rest of them have educational qualifications below sixth standard. All of them are above 50 years of age.

Trustees

There are five trustees. According to the constitution, the trustees are elected after 10 years. In actual practice, this is not strictly followed. Usually elections are conducted after 15 or 20 years. If one makes a historical analysis of the trustees it is clear that most of the posts of trustees are the monopoly of certain families. All the trustees are over 50 years of age and their educational qualification is below seventh standard.

In addition to trustees there is an advisory committee of three members to give guidance to the executive members for the proper functioning of the panch committee. Those persons who had assumed important position like Sarpanch or President in the panch committee are usually preferred as advisory committee members.

One of the important functions of this panchayat is to sanction the marriages of its members. At the time of marriage, as a token of respect, *Tikka* and *Pansupari* are given to the "Peddamanshis". Earlier all marriages were sanctioned by "Peddamanshis", but today the president also does this duty. Rules of endogamy are very strict. Members are ex-communicated if they contract an intercaste marriage. But they can come back as full-fledged members after paying certain amount as fine.

A well-organized "Nyaya Committee" is looking after the judicial problems. Any sorts of disputes, problems regarding engagement and marriage, and property rights are settled by the "Nyaya Committee". Even now "Peddamanshis" plays a prominent role in settling the judicial matters. According to the president almost all the judicial matters are settled in the panchayat itself. This is because of the heavy expenses and the lengthy procedure that are involved in the law courts that the members prefer to settle their problems in the panchayat itself. Moreover the members also think that if they take a matter to court it is an insult to their leaders.

In addition to the above mentioned types of functions, the panch committee has also taken up educational, religious and other social welfare activities. Some of the functions, such as educational and religious work, have been undertaken by separate association which are under the control of this panchayat. This panchayat owns three temples, one *Mangal Karyalaya*, one *ashram* and a *dharmashala* at Alandi.

Example II

Telugu Madelwar Samaj, Kirkee

During the early decades of 20th century, the locality where the Telugu Madelwars residing in Pune was known as "third". There were five "thirds": (1) Sholapur bazaar, (2) Sadar Bazaar, (3) Camp, (4) Kirkee (including Cyprus and Ghorpadi) and (5) Mothikhana. Each third had its own 'Chowdhary' and functioned as an independent panchayat. In each third the 'Chowdhary' was responsible for managing the community activities. The 'Chowdharys' misused the income of the respective thirds, that they get at the time of marriage and as subscription fees. They had spent the income of the panchayat on drinks; moreover, they had not kept any record of the income. Later all the five thirds fused together and formed a common panchayat known as "Brigade". There was one representative from each third. Among them one acted as the chief. This "Brigade" acted as a common panchayat for all the thirds. If there was some dispute or marriage or engagement problem between the thirds, then the chief, alongwith the Chowdharys' of the respective thirds, came together and settled the matter. The majority of the Telugu Madelwar Community members were staying at the Kirkee Cantonment area, and they found it very difficult to go up to Camp to attend the meetings and functions organized by the "Brigade". Since the Kirkee area had the maximum number of members, they started keeping the monthly subscription amount separately. This created resentment among the leaders in the Camp area. And the leaders in the Camp made it compulsory for members to wear a *dhoti* and *kurtha* while attending each and every function organized by the 'Brigade'. Because of these reasons, in 1930, the members who came from the Kirkee dominion, including Ghorpadi and Cyprus, split off from the "Brigade" and started their own panchayat at Kirkee. Today Telugu Madelwar Community members in Pune have two panchayats, one at Kirkee and the other at Camp, and both of them work independently.

Telugu Madelwar Samaj at Kirkee was started in 1930 under the leadership of Mr. Laxman, who was the representative from Kirkee third to the Brigade. In 1934 it was rearranged by a new head who was known as "Chowdhary" and four Committee members. During the initial stages the main aim of this panchayat was to help the members to arrange their marriage, to curtail the marriage expenses, and to help the members at the time of funerals. At that time marriage ceremonies lasted about seven days. In 1936, it was reduced to three days. Until the 1950s they collected membership fees from each member at the rate of Re.0.50, and membership was compulsory for all married males and females. From 1977 onwards they increased this amount to Re.1 per head. Until 1952 the post of 'Chowdhary' was hereditary even though the committee members' posts were not. A selected member could continue in same post until his death.

In 1952 the association prepared rules and regulations and registered this panchayat under the Charitable Trust. Today the official body is partially democratic. The president's post is always reserved for the eldest and the most respected persons in the community. Office bearers consist of the president, the secretary, and nine committee members. The present president is uneducated and his duties are limited. Most of his duties are carried out by the secretary. The majority of committee members are young. Even though they have written rules and regulations, in practice they do not follow them strictly. There is no fixed time for the election of office bearers, even though it is clearly specified in the constitution. The last election they had was in 1977. Office bearers are elected in the general body meeting.

Committee meetings are fixed on 11th of every month. Meetings are arranged in the temple premises or in the President's house. A messenger is assigned the duty of informing the members regarding the functions or meeting arranged by the panchayat.

The main function of this panchayat is to sanction marriage of the members and to settle any sort of judicial problems among the members. The president sanctions marriages and takes active part in settling judicial cases. They celebrate most of the Hindu festivals, such as *Ganesh Chaturthi*, *Ganesh Festivals*, *Ashadha Jatra*, etc. There is one Pochamma temple under the jurisdiction of this panchayat. The temple hall is used for arranging marriages of its members. Earlier this panchayat celebrated national festivals, such as August 15, and January 26. Recently they have stopped.

TYPE III : DIFFERENTIATED

Authority Structure

This type of panchayat is managed exclusively by the younger persons between the ages of 30 to 40. Authority has been transferred from the older members to younger ones. A purely democratic set up of the official body exists in this panchayat. Both panchayats which come under this category are registered and have written rules and regulations. They follow the rules and regulations strictly to a certain extent in the actual behavioural pattern.

Regulation of Marriage

The rules of endogamy are not very strict. However, marriage is sanctioned by the president, and payment of marriage cess is compulsory. It varies from Rs. 20 to Rs. 51 for boys and Rs. 20 to Rs. 37 for girls. In this type of panchayat, if the members contract inter-caste marriage they are not punished. However, the number of inter-caste marriage in these panchayats is negligible.

Judicial Functions

The panchayats of this category take little interest in settling the judicial matters within the panchayat. A well defined "Nyaya Committee" is absent. Even if there is a serious case, such as divorce or marital adjustment problems, the president collects a certain amount of money as fine and sends them to court

Level of Organization

Defined Decision-Making

In both panchayats printed and defined decision-making processes are present in their constitution.

Specified Meeting

Meetings are specified in both panchayats. Committee meetings and general body meetings are specified.

Specified Organizational Activity

In addition to sanctioning marriage, these panchayats have also taken up educational and social welfare activities which are specified in the constitution.

Defined Activities for Office Bearers

The duties of the office bearers are defined in the constitution and are followed by both panchayats.

Registration and Written Rules and Regulations

Both panchayats are registered and have written rules and regulations. They follow the rules and regulations strictly to a larger extent.

Record Keeping

Both of them keep records and documents regarding the panchayat activities. Since neither panchayat has an office, all documents are kept with the president of the respective panchayats.

Defined Criteria for Membership

Membership in both panchayats is given at the sub-caste level. Membership is ascribed by birth. Criteria of membership are defined in the constitution in both cases.

Level of Activity

Presence of General Body Meeting

Once a year both the panchayats conduct a general body meeting.

Committee Meeting

Both panchayats conduct atleast one committee meeting each month, although it may increase to two per month. Committee meetings are held usually on Sundays.

Collection of Membership Fee

Telugu Shimpi Samaj at Dargigalli stopped collecting the membership fee. The president informed us that they stopped it because the office bearers do not get time to go from door to door to collect it. But the members are ready to pay the same. Till 1976 they collected the membership fee at the rate of Re.1 from the head of the household on a monthly basis. Telugu Munnurwar Jynatha Ganga at Kirkee collects monthly subscription from the head of the household at a rate of Rs.2 per month.

Exercise of Common Property

Telugu Munnurwar Jynatha Ganga at Kirkee does not have common property of its own, whereas the latter has a building whose hall is used for arranging marriage of its members.

Exercise of Common Fund

The main source of income of these panchayats comes from marriage cess and membership fees. The monthly income of these panchayats is around Rs. 200 to Rs. 300.

Level of Democratization

Initial Selection of Office Bearers

A well-organised democratic type of official body is present. Office bearers are elected democratically in a general body meeting.

Participation of Members in Election

Members participate actively to elect the office bearers. All the office bearers are elected in the general body meeting.

Regular Election

Elections are conducted according to written rules in the constitution. The office bearers of Telugu Munnurwar Jynatha Ganga at Kirkee are elected every three years and those of Telugu Shimpi Panchayat at Dargigalli every year.

General Participation in Decision-Making

In both panchayats democratic type of decision-making process take place. Members are actively involved in decision-making processes.

Division of Labour among Office Bearers

Each of the office bearers is assigned his own area of work and the duties are clearly defined in the constitution. Each one is responsible for performing his own assigned task.

In order to show the dynamic changes that are observed in the differentiated type of panchayat, two cases are presented. Both panchayats have undergone considerable structural and functional adaptation. The most remarkable change undergone by them is that the authority structure has been transferred from the older generations to the younger generations, and both panchayats are managed by younger generation. The office bearers are elected purely on a democratic basis. They have reduced the major functions of the traditional caste panchayat and have added functions such as educational, and social welfare.

Example I

Telugu Shimpi Samaj : Dargigalli

The Shimpis who migrated from Telangana district of Nizam dominion are mainly concentrated at Kirkee and Pune Cantonment areas. Till 1932 the Shimpis in Pune had one common panchayat which was situated at Kirkee. Since the distance between Camp and Kirkee is rather long, members staying at Camp found it difficult to go to Kirkee to attend the functions and meetings arranged by the panchayat. Thus the people at Camp started their own panchayat in 1932.

Till 1952, this panchayat was managed by a panch committee. The panch committee members are selected from those elderly persons from the community. The posts of panch committee were hereditary and in some cases, the post is continued till the death of the panch. The panch committee members did not maintain any accounts. Whatever money they got from the members they misused for their personal purposes. In those days the main function of panch committee was to sanction the marriage of its members and regulate their behaviour.

In order to save the income for constructive and welfare activities, in 1943, they formed a trust with the following intention: (1) to construct a house for the Samaj and (2) to stress the importance of education among the children by giving them some sort of incentives, such as scholarships and books.

In 1952 this panchayat prepared rules and regulations and registered itself. Even after registration this association was managed by elderly persons in the community. A decade ago, the younger generation took over the panchayat. After that they started a democratic type of official body. The executive committee members are the president, vice-president, secretary, joint secretary and two treasurers. In addition there are 11 committee members. Executive Committee members are elected every year. The office bearers and committee members are elected in the general body meeting. This panchayat is managed by younger persons between the ages of 30 to 40. The educational qualifications of the office bearers and committee members are matric and above, except one, who is non-matric. This panchayat mostly follows rules and regulations in all activities.

Today the main function of this panchayat is to sanction the marriage of its members and provide other social welfare activities. Its function as a judicial system is almost gone. The panchayat has a building of its own. The building hall is used for arranging marriage of its members. Cooking vessels, carpets, and glasses, are available for the members on rental basis for functions. Every year books worth Rs.1,000 are distributed among the students. Competitions such as essay-writing, debates, athletics for boys and *rangoli* and embroidery for girls are also arranged. Recently they stopped arranging religious festivals.

Example II

Kirkee Munnurwar Jynatha Ganga Trust, Kirkee

Munnurwars are concentrated in Rastapeth, Laskhar, Sholapur bazaar, Shukrawar Peth, Kirkee, Cyprus and Vaithalwadi. For a long time each of these localities had independent panchayats which were managed by a "Chowdhary". In each panchayat the respective "Chowdhary" was responsible for the management of the panchayat and regulating the behaviour of the members. Recently the nearby Jynatha Gangas amalgamated and today there are four Jynatha Gangas. In 1955 Lashkar and Sholapur bazaar Jynatha Gangas amalgamated into Lashkar-Sholapur bazaar Jynatha Ganga. Kirkee, Cyprus and Vaithalwadi Jynatha Gangas amalgamated into Kirkee Munnurwar Jynatha Ganga trust. This fusion took place in 1979. The other two

Jynatha Gangas are working independently.

For quite a long time the Munnurwars staying at Kirkee, Cyprus and Vaidalwadi had their own panchayat, which worked independently. In these panchayats the "Chowdhary" was selected from certain families such as Poonam, Gandham and Lucka. And whatever income they got from the panchayats went into the pocket of the respective "Chowdharys". In order to stop the monopoly of these families, to collect the income of the panchayat systematically, to utilize the income for the welfare of the community, and to give opportunities to younger generations to manage the community under the leadership of Dr. Gandham the Kirkee Munnurwar Jynatha Ganga was formed by amalgamating all three nearby Jynatha Gangas. The major aim of this panchayat is to bring their community members together, to make them know each other, help them at the time of marriage, work for the welfare of the community, and to help the poor students of the community in education and sports. In the year of its foundation they registered it by preparing the rules and regulations. This association, like the former one, is fully managed by the younger generations. The present official body consists of the president, vice-president, secretary and treasurer and auditor. In addition to the office bearers there are six committee members. Two are nominated from "Akhil Bharathiya Munnurwarlu Sanghtna" by its president. This is an association among the Munnurwars in Pune, which is working at the Maharashtra level with branches all over the State. The educational qualifications of the office bearers are above matric, and all of them are between 30 and 45. All the office bearers and committee members are elected in the general body meeting.

As with the first one, its function as a judicial system is almost gone and the celebration of religious festivals has stopped completely. The Panchayat distributes books and provides tuition fees to poor and needy students.

From the above discussions the major characteristic features of the three types of panchayats are drawn as follows:

Fused

1. Indigenous in origin and exhibiting almost all the characteristics of traditional village caste panchayat with the least adaptation to the changing urban scene.
2. Marriage is sanctioned by the panchayat for its members and

the payment of marriage cess is compulsory.

3. Rules of endogamy are very strict. If any member enters the inter-caste marriage, he/she is punished or ex-communicated.
4. Judicial functions are very strong. All matters regarding cases are settled within the panchayat itself. In this type the president himself, or in some cases, the president with the help of committee members, looks after judicial matters.
5. Traditional type of authority, as in the village caste panchayat, is prevalent in this type. In a few panchayats the presidential post is hereditary. Still in others presidential post is reserved for an elderly person in the community.
6. All panchayats are not registered and do not have any written rules and regulations. Meetings are not fixed and no general body meeting takes place. Committee meetings are held in the president's house, usually at night when committee members are free from their work.
7. Religious, educational and social welfare functions are absent.

Transitional

1. It is indigenous in origin and retains most of the characteristics of the traditional caste panchayat with minimum adaptations to the changing urban conditions.
2. Marriage is sanctioned by the panchayat and payment of marriage cess is compulsory.
3. Rules of endogamy are very strict. Those members who break the rules of endogamy are punished.
4. A well organized "Nyaya Committee" is found in almost all the panchayats. The "Chowdhary" or president takes active part in settling the judicial matters. Office bearers take special care to settle the members' judicial problems within the panchayat itself. In a few cases, if the case is minor such as disputes or personal problems committees may not take much interest. But if the case is major such as divorce or marital adjustment, the "Nyaya Committee" considers the case.
5. Here democratic authority has been superimposed upon the traditional type of authority. Still the traditional type of authority dominates. The traditional and democratic methods of selection of office bearers co-exist. Important posts, such as the president, and vice-president are reserved for elderly persons in

the community. The younger generation is preferred mainly for committee members posts. Committee meetings and general body meetings are present.

6. Except for two cases, the rest of this category have written rules and regulations and are registered. But no panchayat strictly follows the rules and regulations as written in the constitution.
7. The panchayats undertake religious, educational, and social welfare functions.

Differentiated

1. It is indigenous in origin and most of the characteristics of traditional caste panchayat are atrophied for better adaptation to the changing urban situation.
2. Marriage is sanctioned by the panchayat for the members and the payment of marriage cess is made compulsory.
3. Rules of endogamy are not very strict, as seen in the case of the last two types of panchayats. If a member enters into an inter-caste marriage, he is not punished. But the number of inter-caste marriages in this panchayat is very negligible.
4. Judicial functions are almost absent. A well-organized "Nyaya Committee" is also absent. The office bearers take little interest in settling the judicial problems of its members. Usually the president direct the members to the court to have their judicial problems solved.
5. Authority system is purely democratic. This panchayat in fully managed by the younger generation. Authority has been transferred from the older members to the younger members. No particular criteria are required for those who stand for the office bearers posts, as seen in the first two cases. All executive committee members are elected in the general body meeting.
6. All the panchayats are registered and have written rules and regulations. They follow the rules and regulations as written in the constitution to a larger extent.
7. Additional functions, such as educational and other social welfare activities, are undertaken by them. Both panchayats have stopped celebrating religious festivals. The functions are changing from instrumental to instrumental expressive.

Conclusions

It is observed elsewhere that with increasing western education, establishment of courts of law, the Special Marriage Act of 1923, and modernizing factors the importance of caste panchayats in the village as well as in the urban contexts is decreasing. The analysis of data on twenty caste panchayats in the industrializing city of Pune shows that despite various factors, such as industrialization and urbanization, caste panchayats are not disappearing or breaking down but, are being modified according to the changing situations. Historical analysis of twenty caste panchayats in the city of Pune shows that all of them started as traditional village caste panchayats. During various stages of development they have undergone changes or modifications in order to cope with the changing situation. In the process of development a few associations have undergone fusion and fission at sub-caste level at various stages.

Out of the twenty caste panchayats, six (Fused) have retained all the characteristics of the traditional caste panchayats without undergoing much adaptation in their structure and function. Twelve of them (Transitional) are in a transitional stage, where traditional and modern elements co-exist. In the remaining two (Differentiated) most of the traditional characteristics have atrophied.

The overall analysis shows that the majority of them is in a stage of transition which we expect, since a country like India is one of the biggest transitional societies in the world. The data further show that the association which is based on traditional forms of sodalities are not disappearing or being replaced by secondary ties in the Indian urban context. The reasons may be because the sodalities inherent in the caste panchayat still performs important primary group functions. Another reason may be that the caste panchayat is the main basis by which ethnic identity of caste members is preserved in the urban setting. Moreover, the ethnic groups under study are economically and educationally backward. Even today caste members stick to their panchayats to satisfy to some extent their social, economical, religious and cultural needs.

The forces which are responsible for the changes in the caste panchayats may be categorized into two: (1) Those which act from within the community and (2) those which act from outside the community. In some communities the educated group started moving against the traditional mode of panchayat functioning. For example, among Padmasalis, younger educated groups recently have formed as association known as "Kruti Samithi" in order to demand radical changes in the present method of functioning. The objectives of this panchayat are: (1) to stop the traditional mode of functioning of caste panchayat, (2) to stop the hereditary "Chowdhary" system, and (3) to give equal representation to the younger generation in the caste panchayat. However, this sort of association could make little impact on the traditional mode of functioning of caste panchayat.

The forces which act from outside are mainly governmental influence and the necessity of registration. Many of the office bearers of different panchayat informed us that they actually do not want to register their association. Once they register it they have to follow certain formalities, such as keeping proper accounts, preparing rules and regulations and democratic set up of office bearers. Even though out of 12 panchayats in the transitional type, 10 are registered, in actual behaviour they do not follow the prescribed formalities of registration.

It is the change in power structure which ultimately results in change in the structure and function of the association. Even though few associations have apparent characteristics of modern organizations, such as registration and democratic type of official body, they are not turning into a modern or voluntary association. Further, the present study do not support the "breakdown" or "transformation" of ethnic association as a result of industrial urbanization.

NOTES

1. Fused panchayats are those which replicate most of the original characteristics of village caste panchayats. Transitional panchayats are in a stage of transition. One of the distinguishing features of transitional panchayat is that the traditional and modern organizational features do co-exist. However, the traditional features are largely projected outside. Differentiated panchayats have incorporated certain modern organizational features. And this ultimately resulted in the partial differentiation of structure and function of caste panchayats for better adaptation to suit the changing condition.
2. For the first two types of panchayats viz. Fused and Transitional, the chief of the panchayat is popularly referred to as "Peddamanshi" or "Chowdhary" or President by its members. We have used "Peddamanshi", "Chowdhary" and president interchangeably, which means the chief of panchayat. The chief of the Differentiated panchayat is popularly referred to only as president by its members.

4

ETHNIC ASSOCIATIONS AND THEIR ADAPTIVE FUNCTIONS

Current emphasis in anthropological studies on the role of ethnically based associations is directed at societies undergoing rapid social-economic and political change. Urbanization and industrialization, call for migration of people from villages and other cultural regions to cities. In order to meet the exigencies of the city life migrants from various types of associations in the city. Many attempts have been made by various scholars to classify these associations on the basis of their function. Rose Arnold (1954) classified them into two categories based on their function. They are social influence groups, and expressive groups. Social influence groups are those which wish to achieve some conditions or change in some segments of society or even the whole society, whereas expressive groups, only express or satisfy the interest of their members in relation to themselves. Following Rose, Nicholas (1959) proposed a threefold classification viz. instrumental, expressive and an intermediate stage of instrumental-expressive.

Studies on the adaptive functions of ethnically based associations in the anthropological literature can be categorized into two. They are Cross Sectional (classificatory) and longitudinal (over time perspective). Many cross sectional studies are available on the adaptive functions of ethnic associations especially in the Asian, African and Latin American countries. But studies which emphasis on the adaptive functions overtime are very scanty. A few attempts have been made in the African and Western contexts. In the African context Southall (1969:38) showed that the tribal associations pass through three different phases. In the first phase the tribal associations are formed on the basis of kinship and tribal bonds which is used for mutual aid. The second phase is in which the tribal bonds to form associations for common interest. In the western context Price (1975) has analysed the changing aspect of U.S. and Canadian urban ethnic institutions over time and showed that they are formed in four successive stages and each stage is dominated by institutions of particular type. His model also shows that there is a shifting of associations from informally organized bar cliques and personal networks to a more formally organized institutions. He further showed that as the ethnic institution advances, their functions also change.

Since no systematic studies on the sequence of development of ethnic associations are available in the Indian context, the present chapter tries to fill the lacuna. This chapter attempts to study the changing role of ethnic associations over time among the immigrants by analysing the adaptive features in their structure and function from a longitudinal perspective. Considering the present status and by assessing the structural and functional adaptations undergone by them over time, these associations have been categorized into four stages of development. They are: (1) Active, (2) Passive, (3) Transformed and (4) Disbanded. Active associations are those which have retained their original structure and functions. Some associations of this type have taken up new functions in addition to the original one. Associations which are atrophied most of their original structure and functions are called passive associations. They are passive because the need or importance of these associations has been discounted due to the changing needs of the society. Transformed associations are those in which the original structure and functions have atrophied and they have taken over new form and content. Disbanded associations are those which are already dead and not functioning at present.

Associations are formed by the immigrants in the city to attain certain goals. Depending upon the need, the types of associations formed vary from society to society. A society which is fast changing may have different types of associations to meet its changing needs. Once the intended function of the association is achieved it may become passive and ultimately it may die off. On the other hand in certain circumstances some associations which are active suddenly get disbanded. Yet in other cases, the passive association may transform themselves into another form depending upon the need of the society. The life span of these associations is determined by the society. All the associations need not go through all the four stages. Some of them may die off soon and others may retain their structure and function for quite a long time. Identification of associations in each stage will help us to study the change in function and the development of associations over time.

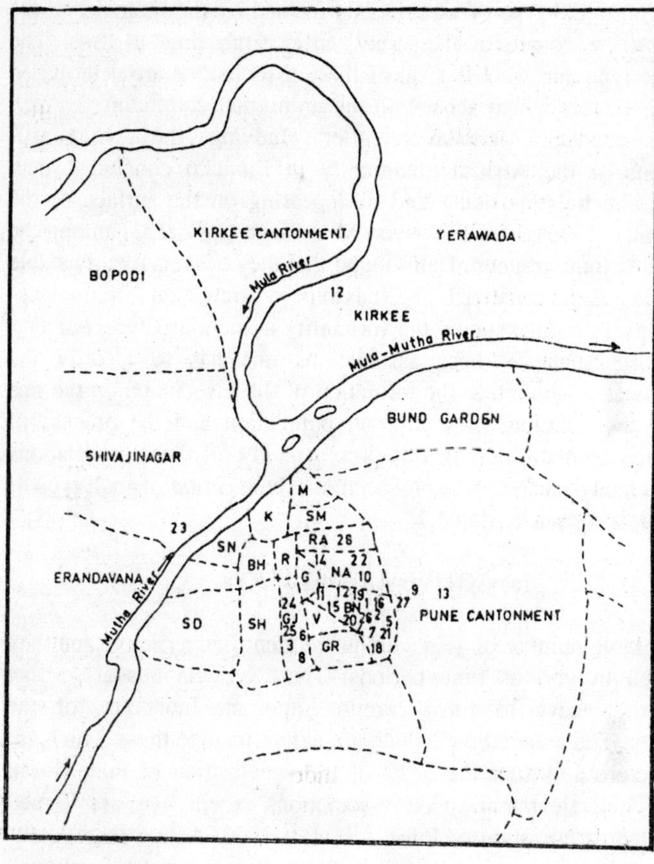

MAP 4.1: Map showing locations of active associations

Notes:

1. Padmasali Shikshnotejak Samastha, Bhavanipeth
2. Gita Granthalaya, Bhavanipeth
3. Poona Handloom Weavers Cooperative Society, Ganjpeth
4. Sreenivas Co-operative Society, Bhavanipeth
5. Powerloom Cooperative Society, Bhavanipeth
6. Balaji Co-operative Society, Ganjpeth
7. Saraswathi Co-operative Society, Bhavanipeth
8. Markhandeya Co-operative Society, Ganjpeth
9. Kamathipura Sarvajanik Ganesh Mandal, Camp
10. Andhra Jharale Tarun Mandal, Nanapeth
11. Padmasali Mitra Mandal, Bhavanipeth
12. Dhobi Darjigalli Tarun Mandal, Camp
13. Telugu Dhobi Tarun Mandal, Camp
14. Jaya Bajarang Mandal, Nanapeth
15. Vikas Tarun Mandal, Bhavanipeth
16. Ashok Tarun Mandal, Bhavanipeth
17. Sree Padmasali Markhandeya Bhajan Manda. Bhavanipeth
18. Padmasali Sreenivas Bhajan Mandal, Bhavanipeth
19. Padmasali Mahila Bhajan Mandal, Bhavanipeth
20. Vaidik Satsang Mandal, Bhavanipeth
21. Yogeshwar Swadhaya Kendra, Bhavanipeth
22. Padmasali Bhavanarishi Samaj Seva Sangh, Nanapeth
23. Andhra Association, Deccan Gymkhana
24. Rashtriya Shivankala Kamgar Sabha, Ganjpeth
25. Vinkar Sahakari Graha Rachana Samstha, Ganjpeth
26. Markhandeya Housing Society, Bhavanipeth
27. Telugu Mochi Co-operative Society, Camp
28. Munnurwar Housing Society, Rastha Peth

The nature and type of associations formed by the migrants in the city during the course of their stay varies from time to time. The nature, the type and the life span of these associations are determined by various factors which act within the immigrant community as well as from outside. Meillassoux after studying the "voluntary" associations of the African community in Bamako concluded that, "they are like bubbles rising and disappearing on the surface of the boiling water" (1968:147). However, Mrs. Singh (1975:103) among the South Indian immigrants in Delhi found that they are remarkably stable over time and criticized Meillassoux's view on "voluntary" associations. In order to study the variability in their structure, function and the life span of these associations one has to identify the circumstances which led to the formation of the association on the one hand and the structure of immigrant population and the process of urbanization on the other. In this present study all these associations have been analysed from this prospective. The location of each type of association is shown in Map 4.1.

(a) ACTIVE ASSOCIATION

A considerable number of associations are identified as active and they are formed in various time periods. These associations are active because they have to fulfil certain important functions for the community. The associations which are active include those which are formed before and after the onset of industrialization of Pune. From Table 4.1 it is clear that all the associations except five, are formed after the industrialization of Pune, i.e. after 1950. Active associations have been classified under the following headings, viz. : Educational, religious, youth, co-operative societies and regional associations.

I. **Educational Associations**

Various measures have been taken by the immigrants to promote education among them. This is attempted by establishing educational institutions as well as by giving incentives like scholarships and other items of stationery to the students. Most of the lower caste communities under study help their students financially as well as by giving books and other items of stationery. The Padmasali community is one such educationally backward community and the population of this particular community is quite large. The members of this community felt a need to start a separate association for promoting education among them, and thus the Padmasali Shikshnotejak Samastha was established by the Padmasali Panch Committee.

TABLE 4.1: Active Associations with the Year of Foundation and Type

Name of the Association	Year of foundation	Type
I. *Educational Association*		
1. Padmasali Shikshnotejak Samastha, Bhavanipeth	1961	Instrumental
2. Gita Granthalaya, Bhavanipeth	1974	Instrumental
II. *Youth Associations*		
1. Kamathipura Sarvajanik Ganesh Mandal, Camp.	1900	Instrumental Expressive
2. Andhra Jharale Tarun Mandal, Nanapeth	1944	Expressive
3. Padmasali Mitra Mandal, Bhavanipeth	1950	Expressive
4. Dhobi Dargigalli Tarun Mandal, Kirkee	1968	Expressive
5. Jaya Bajarang Mandal, Nanapeth	1976	Expressive
6. Telugu Dhobi Tarun Mandal, Camp	1978	Expressive
7. Ashok Tarun Mandal, Bhavanipeth	1978	Expressive
8. Vikas Tarun Mandal, Bhavanipeth	1981	Expressive
III. (a) *Co-operative Societies; Housing Co-operative Societies*		
1. Vinkar Sahakari Graha Rachana Samastha, Ganjpeth	1962	Instrumental
2. Markhandeya Housing Society	1978	Instrumental
3. Telugu Mochi Co-operative Society, Camp.	1981	Instrumental
4. Munnurwar Housing Society, Rasthapeth	1982	Instrumental
(b) *Handloom Co-operative Societies*		
1. Poona Handloom Weaver Co-op. Society, Ganjpeth	1947	Instrumental
2. Powerloom Co-operative Society, Ganjpeth	1975	Instrumental
3. Saraswathy Co-operative, Bhavanipeth	1978	Instrumental
4. Sreenivas Co-operative Society, Bhavanipeth	1980	Instrumental
5. Balaji Co-operative Society, Ganjpeth	1980	Instrumental
6. Markhandeya Co-operative Society, Ganjpeth	1982	Instrumental
IV. *Community Welfare Association*		
1. Rashtriya Shivan Kala Kamgar Sabha, Ganjpeth	1980	Instrumental
2. Padmasali Bhavanarishi Samaj Seva Sangh, Nanapeth	1962	Instrumental Expressive
V. *Religious Associations*		
1. Padmasali Mahila Bhajan Mandal, Bhavanipeth	1945	Expressive
2. Vaidik Satsang Mandal, Bhavanipeth	1974	Expressive
3. Padmasali Sreenivas Bhajan Mandal, Bhavanipeth	1977	Expressive
4. Sri Padmasali Markhandeya Bhajan Mandal, Bhavanipeth	1980	Expressive
5. Yogeshwar Swadhaya Kendra, Bhavanipeth	1962	Expressive
VI. *Regional Association*		
1. Andhra Association, Deccan Gymkhana	1941	Instrumental Expressive

Padmasali Shikshnotejak Samastha

The association was inaugurated by Shri P.P. Battin at Alandi in June 1961. The Padmasali Panch Committee collected contribution from the community members as well as from company owners in Pune. A major contribution was given by Padmasali Panch Committee itself. By 1974 the capital of the association rose to Rs. 32,000 out of which Rs. 10,000 had been deposited with the Panch Committee. During the year 1974-78 owing to the mismanagement of the association they ran at a lose. By 1978 the balance came down to Rs. 14,000. The same year Mr. S.N. Kunden took charge of the association. He withdrew the deposit of Rs. 10,000 from the Panch Committee and gave it to some traders on the basis of interest, and worked hard to raise the capital. In June 1980 they also received Rs. 5,500 from the Municipal Corporation. Today the main source of income is membership fee as well as the contribution they get from the caste members at the time of their marriage. It is a norm in the community that at the time of marriage the bride and groom pay a certain amount of money to the association. There are altogether 250 life members. Life membership fee is Rs. 51 per member. There is no ordinary membership.

On 5th September, 1980 the association got registered under the Bombay Public Trust Act by forming a trust. There are eight trustee members and they are elected every three years. The office bearers consist of a president, vice-president, secretary, joint secretary, treasurer and an internal auditor. The Panch Committee nominate the Chairman and the Secretary and the rest of the office bearers are elected.

Activities

From its very inception this association has been supplying books and scholarships to poor and deserving students in the community. In 1980 they awarded scholarships of Rs. 25 to College going students and the following year this amount was raised to Rs. 35. In 1981 they distributed books worth Rs. 8,000.

Padmasali Shikshnotejak Samastha Balwadi

In 1974 with the help of Panch Committee this association started two nurseries one in Bhavanipeth and the other in Ganjpeth in order to give primary education primarily to the children of their community. However, admission is given to children of other communities as well. In both the nurseries medium of instruction is Marathi. In 1979 the nursery at Ganjpeth was closed due to lack of adequate number of students. In the same year they opened another one at Nanapeth. In Nanapeth, a Marwadi provided a rent free room to run the classes. Majority of the students in these two Balwadis are Padmasalis, who are residing in Bhavanipeth, Nanapeth and Ganjpeth. For quite some time the number of students did not cross 40. During the past two years there is a tremendous increase in the number of students in both the nurseries.

Sree Markhandeya Prathmik Telugu School

A primary school was started by Pune Municipality in 1926, in order to give education to a large number of Telugu students residing in Pune. The school is located in Bhavanipeth, where the Padmasalis are concentrated. Classes up to fifth standard have been started and the medium of instruction is Telugu. From third standard onwards, Marathi is taught as a second language. In 1981 there were altogether 200 students, distributed as follows. First Standard – 69, Second Standard – 56, Third Standard – 35 and Fourth Standard – 27 and 13 for fifth standard. All the students are of Telugu origin and not even a single Maharashtrian student is identified. Except one Telugu Kshatriya Brahmin and two Telugu Christians, all of them belong to Panchamahal Padmasali and Padmasali caste. Most of the students are from Bhavanipeth, Ganjpeth and Nanapeth except a few who come from Poolgate and Kirkee military quarters. All of them hail from economically backward families. Year after year the number of students in the school is declining, because there is no provision to study Telugu after fifth standard, moreover, studying Telugu will not help the immigrants' children to find a job in Pune. Some of the parents send their children to Andhra Pradesh to take further education in Telugu, other join in Hindi or Marathi medium school. Padmasali Shikshnotejak Samastha provides books and sports items to the students who study in this school.

Gita Granthalaya

For some time library facilities were not available for the Padmasalis residing at Bhavanipeth, Nanapeth and Ganjpeth. So in 1974, Sri Venkatacharya Laxmanachari Kandale with the help of the community founded Gita Granthalaya in Bhavanipeth. In 1975 the library was registered under the Public Trust Act. Membership in the library is open to all community members residing in Bhavanipeth, Nanapeth and Ganjpeth. Except a few all the members are Padmasalis. Altogether there are 200 members and majority of them are from Bhavanipeth and Nanapeth. Admission fee is Re.1 with a deposit of Rs. 10 and the monthly subscription fee is at a rate of Rs. 1.50. The library has a collection of books in various languages such as Telugu, Marathi, Hindi and English. Altogether there are 3,000 books which cover secular and non-secular literature. Books are regularly issued out to the members.

II. **Youth Associations**

Numerous youth associations have sprung up especially among the lower caste Telugu immigrant communities. The major intention of these youth associations is to celebrate Ganesh Festival. Ganesh Festival is widely celebrated in Pune during the month of August – September every year. The establishment of Ganesh "Mandal" at the time of Ganesh festival is socio-politically motivated. This was started with the intention of uniting the Maharashtrians politically to demand independence from the British. After Independence, the formation of Ganesh mandal during the festival days is still continuing. Now its aim has changed into socio-religious. Telugu immigrants in Pune have a long tradition of celebrating this festival. As early as 1900, Tilak who was the prime mover visited Kamathipura (Camp) where there was preponderance of Telugu immigrants settled during the initial stages of their migration. He requested the residents to start a Ganesh "Mandal" and explained the need for developing patriotic feeling among the Telugus. Inspired and influenced by the ideals of Tilak, a Telugu immigrant Shri Iranna Balayya Bugdalwar with the help of Telugu immigrants started "Kamathipura Sarvajanik Ganeshostav Mandal" in 1900. This is the oldest youth Mandal identified among the Telugu immigrants. During the initial stages this "Mandal" was mainly managed, by Telugu immigrants residing in Kamathipura. Today various community members including Muslims take active part in running the "Mandal", however a good number of active members are from Telugu immigrant communities. During the festival, the members instal a Ganapati idol at the Hanuman Temple owned by the "Samastha Telugu Manad Panchayat". For the past several years, the Mandal has been distributing books and scholarships to the poor and needy students, who are residing in the neighbourhood irrespective of their caste and creed.

Apart from the Sarvajanik Ganeshostav Mandal, numerous youth "Mandal" are identified especially among the Telugu lower caste communities. Their objectives are numerous including socio-religious and recreational. However, the prime motive is to celebrate Ganesh Festival which is widely celebrated by the Maharashtrian youths. Out of the eight youth "Mandals"; two belong to Telugu Dhobis, they are: (1) Dhobi Dargigalli Tarun Mandal at Kirkee and (2) Telugu Dhobi Tarun Mandal at Camp. One belongs to Panchamahal Padmasalis. Four belong to the Padmasalis. All of them are managed by young men in the age groups of 15 to 35. Out of the total eight Mandals, one is registered and the rest are unregistered. In two, membership is open to all community irrespective of ethnic background. In the remaining, membership is restricted to the respective caste members. If the membership is restricted to a particular caste, at the time of the festival an ad-hoc committee is formed in which representation is given to local community members. All the Mandals celebrate Ganesh festival with great enthusiasm and zeal. During the festival, members of other communities living in the neighbourhood are invited to take part in the function. The Mandals celebrate most of the Hindu religious festivals, regional as well as local. Another important activity of these Mandals is to arrange sports and games where occasionally members of other ethnic groups are allowed to participate. National days like Independence day and the Republic day are also celebrated by these youth organizations.

The characteristic feature of the "Mandal" is that it is found only among the youths of the early Telugu immigrants. No Mandal is identified among the recently migrated educated Telugu immigrants. The Mandals are popular among the Padmasalis, Panchmahal Padmasalis and Dhobis. It is because the members of these committees are concentrated in certain areas. Other lower caste Telugu immigrants do not have youth Mandals. However, they also celebrate the festival in temples owned by them. During these occasions descendants of the early immigrants interact informally with the locals forgetting their ethnic identity. Sports and games organized by the youth Mandals help the youth to spend their leisure time and to interact informally with other community members of the same age group. Opportunities to the locals to participate in the activity of these youth associations contribute to the integration of the ethnic community with the local population. Thus these Mandals by celebrating local and regional religious festivals and by arranging sports and games not only help to maintain separate ethnic identity but also integrate the community into the multi ethnic urban society. The present study shows that youth Mandals perform important integrative functions.

III. Co-operative Societies

(a) *Co-operative Housing Societies*

Caste based co-operative societies are one of the basis by which caste provides welfare service to its members. Four co-operative housing societies have been identified. They are: Markhandeya Housing Society, Vinkar Sahakari Graha Rachana Samithi, Mannurwar Housing Co-operative Society and Telugu Mochi Co-operative Society. The first two co-operative societies belong to Padmasalis and the other two belong to Mannurwar and Telugu Mochi community respectively. Membership in the co-operative societies is restricted to its own caste members. In the case of Vinkar Sahakari Graha Rachana Samithi membership is given to Padmasalis as well as Panchamahal Padmasalis. All the co-operative societies have acquired land in the suburbs of the city and construction is still in an embryonic stage. Out of the four societies we will discuss one in detail.

The Vinkar Sahakari Graha Rachana Samithi was formed on co-operative basis under the leadership of Sri Yallappa Chandrayya Anandan in 1962. The aim of the society is to start residential colony cum a powerloom factory on a co-operative basis. Membership in the society is open to all Padmasalis and Panchamahal Padmasalis who are originally from Andhra Pradesh. There are altogether 75 members. Entrance fee is Re.1 per head and the members have to take five shares of Rs. 50 each. An additional amount of Rs. 4,000 is collected from all members for the construction of residential colony. For each member the society intends to provide four looms. According to the president, since it is a residential cum powerloom colony each family can manage four looms. For the construction of the powerloom cum residential colony they have already acquired 10 acres of land at Dhankandi (Pune-Satara Road). The preliminary construction work is in progress.

(b) *Co-operative Handloom Societies*

Traditionally Padmasalis are weavers. During the initial stages of their migration many of them were uneducated and came in search of jobs in handloom industries. During the early 20th century handloom industry flourished in Pune and many of the migrants undertook handloom business in small scale in their houses. The small scale handloom owners were getting raw materials from Marwadi and Gujarati businessmen and the finished products were sold to them at low costs. During the mid 20th century, when there was a high competition between handloom and powerloom, the small scale businessmen found it difficult to get markets for their products. The ordinary weavers could not go to big cities like Bombay, Calcutta and Madras to get raw materials and find market for their products. With the competition between handloom and powerloom the poor weavers faced a very difficult situation. So in order to help the handloom weavers during the mid of 20th century, many cooperative societies were started by Padmasalis in Pune. The aim of these co-operative societies were to help the poor weavers by providing raw materials and finding market for their products. Today there are six co-operative societies including handloom as well as powerloom. All of them are located in Ganjpeth, Nanapeth and Bhavanipeth.

Membership in the co-operative societies is open for all community members. Other immigrants from Andhra Pradesh, Ahmednagar and Vidharba and the local koshtis are also members of these co-operative societies. However, majority of the members are Padmasalis in all the co-operative societies. Almost all the members are from among the people residing in Bhavanipeth, Nanapeth and Ganjpeth. The number of members in them varies from 40 to 200. The rules of enrolment also vary from society to society. In some of the societies members have to take certain number of shares in addition to the entrance fee. All these cooperative societies are registered bodies and have a democratic official set up. A few co-operative societies have their own retail and wholesale shops in Pune. In other cases they send the finished products to other co-operative societies elsewhere in the country. The turn over of these co-operative societies is in lakhs. All the members are given eight per cent bonus every years.

Today the Padmasalis in Pune are not solely dependent on handloom and powerloom industries. Many of them are educated and have started diversifying their occupations. Thus the number of handloom workers from this community is decreasing day by day. However, the majority of the handloom weavers in Pune are from this community. In fact co-operative societies helped the Padmasali migrants to revive the handloom industry in Pune and face the competition from powerlooms.

IV. Community Welfare Associations

Rashtriya Shivan Kala Kamgar Sabha

In addition to handloom weaving Padmasalis in Pune were also involved in beedi making. Even though, considerable number of female folks are still involved in beedi making, a few of them have been showing interest in tailoring jobs. As they are economically backward many of them find it difficult to purchase their own sewing machines. They used to hire machines from shops at a rent of Rs. 30 per month. This association was formed in 15th August, 1980, to help the community members to buy their own sewing machines. Membership was initially restricted only to Padmasalis and Panchmahal Padmasalis. However, later on, it was opened to other community members as well. With the help of bank loans, the president of the association distributes sewing machines to its members. The members are required to clear off their debts on instalment. So far the Sabha has distributed 165 machines to its members. Many of the Padmasalis and Panchmahal Padmasalis residing in Bhavanipeth, Nanapeth and Ganjpeth have availed of the facilities offered by the association. Now the association is trying to fulfil the following objectives:

1. Try to find jobs for the trained tailors in some government institutions.
2. To develop it on the lines of a full-fledged co-operative society.

Padmasali Bhavanarishi Samaj Seva Sangh

Padmasali Bhavanarishi Samaj Seva Sangh was formed in 1945, with the intention of providing some sort of welfare facilities to the Padmasalis residing in Navawada. Membership in this association is primarily meant for the Padmasalis. However membership is also given to other community members residing in this neighbourhood.

This association was registered in 1962 and has a democratic official set up. The office bearers consist of a president, a vice-president, a secretary, a general secretary, a treasurer and a co-treasurer. In addition, there is an advisory committee which consists of six members, all of them are above 60 years of age. The advisory committee members can hold this post till their death.

Welfare Activities and Integrative Functions

The association has undertaken various social welfare activities for the people residing in the Navawada neighbourhood. They arrange "Shramadan" in order to keep the neighbourhood clean and neat. Whenever there is a problem regarding supply of electricity and water, complaints are lodged with the municipal authorities to take immediate action. It also takes active part in solving personal as well as family problems of the people residing in the neighbourhood. If any of the resident fall sick and is not able to meet the hospital expenses, the active members of the association come forward with financial help. Whenever there is any dispute among the people residing in this locality, the association takes active part to settle it among themselves. By performing various community welfare activities, the association tries to integrate the people of different communities residing in that locality.

An analysis of membership shows that out of the total, only two per cent represents outside communities and the rest are Padmasalis. By keeping membership open to other community members the association achieves some integration with the people residing in this locality. However the number of outsiders is negligible.

In 1972, with the help of people residing in the locality, the association has constructed a Hanuman temple. The temple is open for all the community members residing in the neighbourhood. Most of the religious festivals are arranged by the association, which include locally as well as regionally prominent functions. They are "Ganesh festival", "Narali Poornima", "Mahashivratri", "Hanuman Jayanthi", "Markhendeya Jayanthi", "Shiv Jayanthi", "Dahihandi" and "Makar-shankranti". This association has been celebrating Ganesh festival for the last 36 years with great zeal. During the festival days a special "Utsav Committee" is formed in which representation is given to the local community members. During 1978-79, and 1979-80 two local community members were selected in the working committee. *Bhajans* are arranged now and then by inviting bhajan groups from outside. Every year Gita Parayan in Telugu as well as in Marathi are arranged by inviting learned scholars. In addition to religious festivals, national days are also celebrated by them.

Even though the association is primarily meant for the welfare of the Padmasalis residing in Navawada, its activities are also directed to the welfare of all other community members residing in the neighbourhood. By arranging common welfare activities and common religious festivals, the association help to integrate the people residing in the neighbourhood.

V. Religious Associations

Almost all the communities under study are engaged in religious activities. Religious feelings are reinforced in various ways, viz. by constructing temples, arranging bhajans, and by celebrating religious festivals. Most of the communities under study have their own temples for worshipping their favourite deities. A review on the studies of religious associations in the urban setting show that they perform two important functions: (1) they help the immigrants to interact at primary group level by performing religious activities and (2) they help to reinforce ethnic solidarity on the one hand and to integrate the immigrants with the local community on the other. Barnes and Peil (1977) has emphasised the primary group function of religious associations in the urban setting. Nair's (1978) study of religious associations among Tamil immigrants in Pune shows the integrative functions of these associations.

Bhajan Mandals

Three Bhajan Mandals are identified among the Padmasali community and all of them are located in Bhavanipeth. They are (i) Markhandeya Bhajan Mandal, (ii) Shreenivas Bhajan Mandal, and (iii) Padmasali Mahila Bhajan Mandal. The oldest Bhajan Mandal is the Markhandeya Bhajan Mandal which was started as Mahavir Bhajan Mandal in 1930, by a few enthusiastic religious devotees. The objectives of the first two bhajan mandals are to stimulate religious feelings among the community members, to convey the ideals of saints and leaders so that the community member adopt them in their daily life and to make them aware of and understand the importance of brotherhood.

Till 1970's Padmasali Markhandeya Bhajan Mandal was mainly managed by older members of the community. Because of ideological conflict a few younger members of the mandal splintered and started Srinivas Bhajan Mandal in 1977. Unlike the Padmasali Markhandeya Bhajan Mandal, the newly formed group welcomed other community members. Out of the total 12 members two are from the local community. Both the "mandals" have their own offices which have been allotted by the Padmasali Panch Committee. Both the mandals have selected office bearers.

Activities

The mandals arrange weekly 'bhajans' in the Hanuman Temple owned by the Padmasali Panch Committee. Whenever, the committee arranges religious festivals like "Markhandeya Utsav", "Shiv Jayanthi" and "Ganesh Utsav", the mandals arrange *Bhajans* and *Kirtans*. "Bhajans" and "Kirtans" are delivered in various languages viz. Telugu, Marathi, Hindi and Gujarathi. Some of the topics chosen are the teachings of Venkateshwar, Shankar, Markhandeya, Bhagwat Gita, Brammanand, Kabir, Meera Bai and Surdas. Ideals of great leaders are presented in the form of "Bhajans" and "Kirtans". Since they render *Bhajans* and *Kirtans* in various languages and on different topics, people residing in the neighbourhood attend the functions irrespective of the caste and creed. Thus the mandals provide an opportunity for the people living in the neighbourhood to interact informally and socialise in the name of religious activities. In addition, both the mandals arrange "Pravachans" by inviting learned Pandits and Scholars. Their activities are not restricted to Pune. They give programmes in different place like Bombay, Nizamabad and Ahmednagar where their community members are concentrated.

Padmasali Mahila Bhajan Mandal

From morning till evening female members of the Padmasali community are busy with their work and seldom come out of their house. In order to bring them out of their house and encourage them to participate in religious activities, a few Padmasali women started "Padmasali Mahila Mandal Gita Sadan Samaj", in 1945. This mandal arranges "Bhajans", "pravachans", and Gita parayan for the female folks. A learned person, Shri Venkatacharya Laxmanachari reads out stanzas from Indian epics like Bhagwat Gita and Mahabharatha to those who are unable to read. The women repeat and learn them by heart. This mandal helps the women folk to come out of their house and participate in religious activities.

All the religious associations are active among the Padmasali community, who claim a high social origin and tradition. These religious associations especially the Bhajan Mandals help the community to come together and interact freely and informally. To a certain extent they also help to integrate the regional community with the locals.

Bhajan mandals are organised on the basis of the religious tradition of Bhakti cult in Hinduism. Milton Singer (1960) found that the city dwellers in Madras are increasingly turning to Bhakti Marga in preference to Karma Marga. This tendency he attributes to urbanization and industrialization. Among the Padmasalis Bhajan Mandals are the dominant religious associations. Singers' observation appears to be valid in the case of Padmasalis of Pune.

VI. Regional Association

Andhra Association

This regional association was started as Andhra Telugu library by Shri Achantha Kanakaraju on 24th December, 1941. Initially this library was located in stables, and later on shifted to rooms near Fergusson College in Deccan Gymkhana. Subsequently this library was renamed as the "Achantha Seshemamba Telugu Library" named after the founder. On 17th December, 1948, this association was registered as Andhra Association and Achanta Seshemamba Telugu Library. When it was registered as Andhra Association the functions of the association were also diversified. The primary objectives of this association are:

(a) to promote fine arts, sports, literature and science,
(b) to provide various recreational facilities to its members,
(c) to promote cultural affinity between the Andhra and the local population,
(d) to participate in the recognised nation-building activities and to render help of humanitarian nature, to the extent possible and permissible, and
(e) to promote educational facilities and do all that is deemed

necessary and relevant to promote the objectives of the association.

Membership in the association is restricted to only Telugu speaking persons whose origin is from Andhra Pradesh. General membership fee is Re.1 per month. A person who pays not less than Rs. 50 can become a life member and for patronship one has to pay an amount not less than Rs. 100. Today there are 100 life members and 300 ordinary members. The managing committee consists of a president, a secretary, and nine committee members. The committee members are nominated on the advice of the secretary. The president and secretary are elected in the general body meeting. The office bearers are elected every year.

The members of this association are scattered all over the city. This association helps as a meeting place for all the Telugu speaking people who are residing in various parts of the city. It helps them to develop friendship and provides a common meeting place. The office of the association is kept open from 06.30 to 07.30 p.m. Usually the members who are residing nearby areas regularly visit this association and make use of the facilities provided for them. Those who are residing in the suburban areas of the city usually come only for special functions organized by the association. The activities of the association are numerous.

Religious Activities

In Andhra Pradesh few shrines are located in the Seven Hills which form part of the eastern ghats. The temples located in this area are managed by the Tirumala Tirupati Devasthanams (TTD). Among them, Lord Venkateshwara temple is very famous. Pilgrims from all over India visit the temple throughout the year. On seventh June, 1981, Andhra Association in collaboration with Tirumala Tirupati Devasthanam opened TTD information centre in the Andhra Association premises. This Centre was opened in order to help the devotees of Lord Venkateshwara in Pune especially the Telugu immigrants. The centre was formed with the intention of extending the following services to the pilgrims to Tirupathi temple.

(a) Sale of Special Darshan Tickets
(b) Reservation of accommodation in Seven Hills
(c) Sale of publications of the Tirupathi temple

(d) Railway reservations for the journey to Seven Hills and back.

From 1981 to 1983 nearly 80 pilgrims have made use of the facilities rendered by the Centre. They include Telugu immigrants as well as other community members.

In 1978, an idol of Lord Venkateshwara was installed in the association building. Every Saturday evening Lord Venkateshwara Pooja is being performed by an immigrant Brahmin who has profound knowledge in performing the pooja. The members can request the authorities to arrange the Lord Venkateshwara Pooja on their behalf by meeting the expenditure.

Educational Activities

Library: The Andhra Association has a collection of nearly 3,000 books in two languages i.e. Telugu and English. The collection mainly consists of literature and novels. The use of this library is restricted to the members of the Andhra Association. A member has to pay an amount of Rs. 6 as annual subscription fee and a refundable deposit of Rs. 10. Five monthlies, three weeklies, and a Telugu newspaper are being subscribed by this Association.

Andhra School: In 1961, few teachers approached the office bearers of this association to get their permission to start a coaching class for children. Education being one of the important objectives of this association they granted permission for starting a Kinder Garten. By 1970, the strength of students increased to nearly 200. With the intention of helping the immigrants' children, they started an English medium school in the year 1970. The school provides education till the sixth grade. They have now decided to upgrade this secondary school into a high school. The association is at present raising funds for this purpose. Admission to this school, is open to all, but Telugu speaking students are preferred. Provision for studying Telugu is being made in this school. But only those immigrants' who are sure of their return to Andhra Pradesh send their children to study Telugu.

Social Work: During the 1977 Andhra Cyclone, this association collected an amount of Rs. 12,000 and contributed to the Andhra Pradesh Cyclone Relief Fund. This association had also contributed money to flood and famine relief funds of Maharashtra and Gujarat Governments.

Recreational Activities

Various entertainment programmes like regional film shows, Telugu dramas, classical dance, and variety entertainment programmes are arranged by the association for its members. Facilities for sports and games are also available for the members. Members make use of these facilities usually in the evenings. The association owns a TV set, which is used for the entertainment of the members.

The Andhra Association differs from other associations in the following aspects. Andhra Association was formed by a group of educated immigrants who came to Pune recently, who are scattered all over the city. Whereas other ethnic associations were formed by early immigrants or their descendants.

Specialization of associations are seen among the early immigrants. In the case of the recent immigrants most of the socio-cultural and educational requirements are met by one association. Unlike other associations discussed in this chapter which have retained their original structure and function to a great extent, the Andhra association has undergone both structural and functional changes over time. This active association has been taking up new functions in addition to the original one. A historical analysis of this association shows this trend. It was initially started as a library but later on it developed into a full-fledged cultural association. During the initial stages of its inception the association helped the new immigrants in finding jobs and arranging accommodation. These functions are not undertaken any more.

During the initial stages of its inception membership was open to South Indians in general although South Indians other than Andhraites were few in number. A Tamilian was the president of this association from 1942-44. During the early phases of industrialization of Pune, the local Maharashtrians used to treat all immigrants from South as "Madrasis" and illtreat them. In order to make them understand the cultural traditions of the South and to reduce the ethnic antagonism, the association projected the South Indian identity. But when the number of Telugu speaking people increased the association stopped admitting South Indians other than Andhraites. The association started arranging talks by inviting scholars and poets from Andhra Pradesh in order to establish the sub-regional identity for the group. The locals were cordially invited to attend these lectures. As a result in 1954 a Maharashtrian scholar Dujaba Deshmukh took active interest in Telugu language and culture. These talks and lectures helped the locals to come close to the immigrants' and to get a general understanding of Telugu language and culture.

As the number of Telugu immigrants increased, its activities also increased and became diverse. Today this association tries to fulfil all the social and cultural needs of its members. Even though the association was started as an instrumental association, it turned into an instrumental-expressive type in order to meet the changing needs of the immigrants.

According to the Constitution, membership in this association is open to all the Telugu speaking people. However, analysis of membership list shows that it does not represent all the Telugu speaking communities in Pune. There are only very few members who belong to second or third generation of the early lower caste Telugu immigrants in this association. These members are educationally and economically well off. They are primarily from the Padmasali community. Members from other lower caste communities are very few. The total strength of the early immigrants is calculated to be below five per cent of the total members. Analysis of the president and secretaries posts from 1941 to 1983 shows that the association is mainly managed by upper and middle caste members, who are well educated.

TABLE 4.2: Distribution of Presidents and Secretaries of Andhra Association on the basis of caste since 1941

Post	Brahmin	Non-Brahmin	Total
President	37 (68.81%)	16 (30.19%)	53 (100.00%)
Secretary	35 (76.09%)	11 (23.91%)	46 (100.00%)

Table 4.2 shows that although this regional association is intended to represent all Telugu migrants it is controlled by the upper and middle caste Telugu immigrants. The lower caste representation is minimal. Except a Christian who continued in the post of president for two years, all others belong to Hindu community. The non-brahmins mainly belong to the Reddy and Kamma caste groups. The analysis further shows that not a single person from the early lower caste immigrants has been selected for the post of either president or the

secretary since 1941. The data confirms the contentions of one of my informants, a senior person and a leader of the Munnurwar community in Pune. "The Andhra Association is managed and controlled by the upper caste people especially the Brahmins. The official posts are divided among themselves. So far they have not given any representation to the Munnurwar community in the official body. Munnurwars residing in Pune requested the office bearers to construct the Andhra School in Rastha Peth where many Telugu immigrants have settled. But the organising committee of Andhra Association turned a deaf ear towards their request. Due to this reasons not a single Munnurwar is a member of this association."

According to an informant from Telugu Dhobi community who was a former member of the Pune Cantonment, the Andhra association is the association of the Brahmins and the educated class. They are neglecting the lower caste Telugu immigrants. Their activities are directed towards only a group of people, and it is very superficial. They are not broadening their outlook and serving their own people – especially the lower caste communities. Therefore, nobody from the Dhobi community is a member of the association.

A member of the Padmasali community expressed the same sentiment: "it is the association of educated and upper caste people, who have migrated to Pune very recently. From our community a few members have taken membership especially who have acquired money and education. If we go there we can see that people who have motor cars socialize with people of their class only. Nobody wants to talk to us and therefore, we feel isolated".

It appears that this association which claims a broader linguistic regional identity as its basis is essentially organized on the lines of caste and class.

Summary

Numerous associations have been identified as active. They include educational, co-operative societies, youth associations, religious, community welfare, and regional associations. These associations have been formed during various time periods of the immigrants' stay in the city. They include associations which were formed during the initial stages of migration as well as those which have been formed recently. Out of the 28 associations which are categorized as active, five of them are formed during the initial stages of Telugu immigrants' settlement in Pune and the rest 23 are formed during the industrialization of Pune. These associations are active, because they perform certain important functions for the immigrant communities.

The activities of active associations are diverse. Educational associations provide facilities to the children of the immigrants. Efforts are also made to teach children their mother tongue. Large number of caste based co-operative societies are formed to help the immigrants in various ways. Numerous religious associations have also been identified. Religious associations are found to perform integrative functions. Youth associations are not found among the first generation. Youth associations emphasize recreational activities and render integrative functions. Another characteristic of active associations is that they are specialized in certain functions. However, the regional association, which is the only associations identified among the recently migrated people, performs various functions for its members. It tries to fulfil social cultural, religious, educational and recreational needs of its members. All the associations including the regional associations are organized on the basis of caste identity whether they claim the caste identity or not.

The associations which are classified as active are of three types. They are instrumental, expressive and instrumental-expressive. Out of the 28 active associations, 13 represent instrumental, and 12 and three represent expressive and instrumental expressive associations respectively. The manifest functions of active associations are education, social welfare and recreation. They also perform an important integrative function.

(b) PASSIVE ASSOCIATIONS

These associations have passed through an active stage and have at present become passive. This is because these associations have fulfilled most of their intended functions for which they had been formed. Three associations are classified as passive. They were formed when the influx of immigrants to the city was large. All of them were active during the initial stages of the migration and settlement of Telugu speaking people to Pune city. Their main function was to help the new migrants to adapt to the city life. Since these associations have fulfilled their task, their importance has been diminished and in due course of time these associations may either cease to exist or they may take up a new role.

TABLE 4.3: Passive Associations with the Year of Foundation and Type

Case	Name of the Association	Year of Foundation	Type
1.	Samastha Telugu Manad Panchayat	1913	Instrumental
2.	Padmasali Markhandeya Sudharak Sangam (Nizamabad Sangam)	1952	Instrumental
3.	Padmasali Yuvak Mandal	1957	Instrumental

The first association was formed as early as 1913 by a large number of Telugu immigrants who settled in Pune during the colonial regime in India. The other two associations were formed by the Telugu Padmasalis in the 1950's when migration was in large number. All the three associations are instrumental in functions. Now we will analyse each of these associations in order to find out the reasons for passivity. The location of passive association is shown in the Map 4.2 along with disbanded associations.

Case I

The initial phase of migration and settlement of Telugu speaking people to Pune is marked by the emigration of a large number of lower caste groups. They migrated in groups and settled mainly in Pune Cantonment and a few in Kirkee Cantonment. These immigrants represented various caste and communities and of each community there were a few members. Since the number of members in each community was very few, there was no possibility of starting communitywise associations. However, a few communities had caste panchayats which were not properly organised and were not functioning properly. It was therefore, felt that there was a need to form an association based on a broader caste group basis, incorporating all the lower caste communities. Therefore, in 1913 Sri Bolli Karadi Rajanna, Sri Rajanna Puram and Sri Jynana Bodke formed Samatha Telugu Manad Panchayat. The following communities were members of the Manad Panchayat. (1) Munnurwar, (2) Mudrasha, (3) Reddy Kapu, (4) Naikopolu, (5) Merollu, (6) Madelwar, (7) Mangalollu, (8) Gullollu, (9) Mottadwar, (10) Gurudwar and (11) Yadav Gauli and (12) Dimerellu. The members of Manad Panchayat are popularly known as Manadi communities. Among the immigrants there were few upper and middle caste members. However, they were not members of

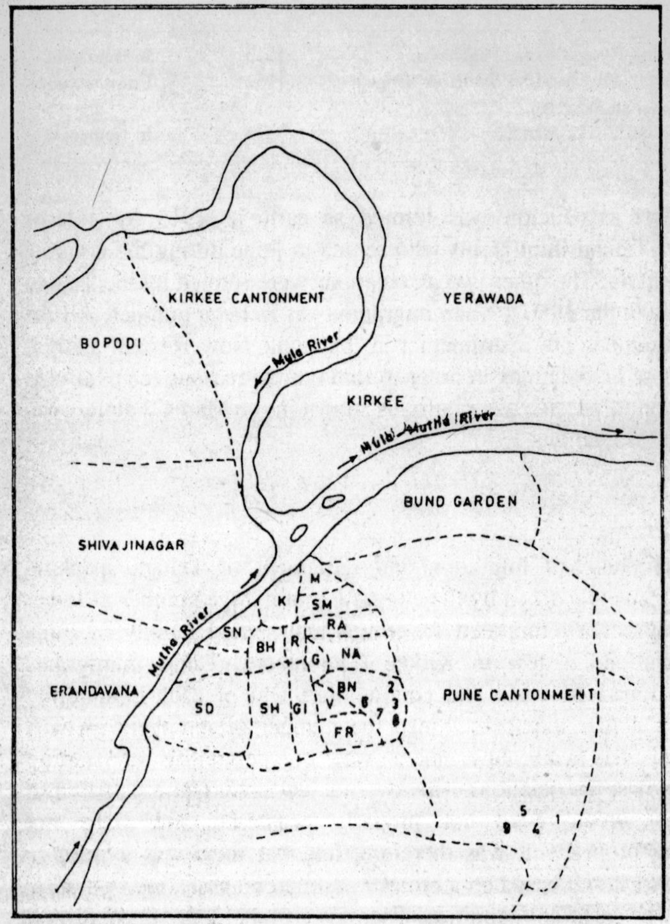

MAP 4.2: Map showing locations of passive and disbanded associations

Notes:

1. Samastha Telugu Manad Panchayat, Camp.
2. Padmasali Markhandeya Sudharak Sangam (Nizamabad Sangam), Bhavanipeth.
3. Padmasali Yuvak Mandal, Bhavanipeth.
4. Telugu Education Fund, Camp.
5. Telugu General Library, Camp.
6. Jyothi Sangam, Bhavanipeth.
7. Markhandeya Mela, Bhavanipeth.
8. Tippiri Mela, Bhavanipeth.
9. Telugu Madelwar Yuvak Mandal, Camp.

the panchayat. This panchayat is formed by a group of people who had similar caste status and common interest. The main function of this panchayat was socio-religious and welfare of the immigrants. Even before 1913 this panchayat was functioning informally. Whenever social, cultural or religious functions were to be arranged, leaders of the different Manadi communities came together and met at temple premises or open places in order to discuss and finalise the matter. In the meeting they used to assign some persons or leaders of the respective communities to collect certain amount as contribution. For such functions, if any of the Manadi community fails to pay the amount after three months of due date, the panchayat had the right to debar that particular community from the Manad panchayat. During the social or religious functions, people from various Manadi communities came together and worked in harmony as members of a single community. For example, during the time of religious or social functions, Gullollu community members sent the message of its members regarding the function, Dapelollu used to beat the drums at the time of marriage and funerals, Dhobis washed cloths for them and carpenters made the idol of God and Goddess during the time of festival. In short, all the community members rendered their respective traditional occupational skills for the proper functioning of the panchayat without accepting any money.

Till, 1926, this panchayat was not well organised. On May 1, 1926, in order to make the panchayat strong, leaders from the Manadi communities called a meeting and decided to take "Chowdharys" from all the Manadi communities. In that meeting they selected Sri Bolli Karadi Rajanna from Munnurwar community as the chief of the Manad panchayat, and 14 "Chowdharys" representing all the Manadi communities were also selected. The decision pertaining Manadi panchayat was taken by the chief in consultation with the "Chowdharys". The posts of the chief and the "Chowdhary" were hereditary from the same family and they could retain their post till their death.

Till 1952 this panchayat was managed by "Chowdharys". On 17.11.1952 Manad panchayat formed a trust of five persons from the following communities viz. Merollu, Reddy Kapu, Gullollu, Munnurwar and Dimerellu and got it registered under the Bombay Public Trust Act 1950. There was no membership fee or regular subscription levied from the members. People belonging to the Manadi communities could make use of the facilities of the panchayat.

Activities

The functions of Manad panchayat were numerous. Its major function was to promote adjustment and adaptation of new migrants to the city life. It helped the members at the time of happy days like marriage and bad days like funerals. The panchayat has taken special care to solve the personal problems of its members. All sorts of regionally prominent religious functions were being arranged by the panchayat. Proper guidance was given to the members to overcome their problems. Requests were also made to the members to abstain from drinks and made them aware of the importance of education. To certain extent the panchayat was functioning as a village caste panchayat.

Judicial Functions

The panchayat acted as a judicial body for the whole community which came under its jurisdiction. Any quarrel or dispute between members within the community or among the communities, were settled by the respective "Chowdharys" amicably. If they failed to do so, a meeting of Manad panchayat was called and the chief in consultation with the "Chowdharys" took the final decision. The decision taken by the chief was final. Problems pertaining marriage and property rights were also undertaken by the panchayat.

Funeral Ceremonies

A burial ground was donated to the Telugu immigrants in Pune by the British. This is located in Gultekdi. This burial ground was managed by the Manad panchayat. Earlier, all the community members who came under this panchayat could bury or cremate their dead in this ground. In 1913, the Manad panchayat divided the burial ground in equal shares to all the communities in order to avoid overlapping and conflict. During the early stages the panchayat collected a nominal charge from the bereaved family for cremating the dead bodies.

During the funeral ceremonies also, the panchayat helped any member physically as well as financially, who was poor and without enough relatives. The usual practice was that in almost all the funeral ceremonies of its members, the chief, most of the "Chowdharys" and members of the panchayat attended the function and rendered assistance.

Marriage Functions

The marriages of members of each community were sanctioned by the respective caste panchayats. However, as a token of respect, it was a custom those days to give *Tikka* and *Pansupari* to all the "Chowdharys" including the chief at the time of marriage of the Manadi community members. Most of the communities had their own caste panchayat which helped in arranging the marriage of its members. If a member was poor the panchayat used to give financial assistance to arrange the marriage.

Religious Activities

As a first step in 1925, Manad panchayat constructed a Hanuman temple in Kamatipura, where the idol of Pochamma Devi was installed. Pochamma Devi is worshipped by all the Manadi communities. In order to construct the temple they got financial assistance from the community members residing in Pune, Sholapur and Bombay. In addition under the jurisdiction of this panchayat there are two more temples. They are Marimata Temple in Babajan Chowk and Pochamma Temple in Taboot street. All the three temples were constructed in Camp where initially preponderance of immigrants settled. The temple halls were given to its members for arranging social functions. Initially most of the regionally predominant Hindu festivals like "Ashad Jatra", "Narali Poornima" and "Buddamma" were arranged by the panchayat.

Pochamma Worship

Pochamma Devi is worshipped by all the Telugu Manadi community members. This Devi worship was largely conducted by Manad panchayat in the month of "Ashad". During this period in the early morning members of Manadi community join together and take out a procession to an isolated forest area to worship the goddess. The females carry pots of water with neem leaves, millet and other cereals in it. After reaching an isolated forest area, they sacrifice buffaloes to the goddess. The meat is cooked and consumed. This was one of the religious festivals celebrated by Manad panchayat with great enthusiasm till the middle of 20th century. Now even though this festival is not celebrated collectively, at community level this occasion is marked by sacrificing goat or hen to the goddess instead of a buffalo.

In addition to the regionally predominant religious festivals, Manad panchayat also used to celebrate other Hindu festivals like "Diwali" and "Holi". During the festivals the chief as well as the "Chowdharys" were given *Tikka* and *Pansupari* to mark the occasion. Most of the religious festivals were arranged collectively in the temple owned by the panchayat. Members from various Manadi communities used to attend the function arranged by the panchayat.

Present Structure of the Panchayat

After the registration of the association, the "Chowdhary" system was abolished and the Panchayat started functioning on democratic lines. When the association was registered, there were five trustees and five office bearers. Today the number of trustees has come down to two. For nearly two decades the posts of the trustee were hereditary and the same family. However, these days nobody takes interest in the trustees post. Today the office bearers consist of a president, a secretary and a treasurer. According to the Constitution of the panchayat the office bearers should be elected every three years. For the past seven years, no election was conducted. Meetings are seldom held, once in a year or once in two years.

Till 1930s, the association was functioning with great zeal and devotion. The migration of lower caste community members increased after the First and Second World War. As the number of members in each community increased, members of the Manad Panchayat started strengthening their own community by uniting all of them at individual caste level. In this way the interest to work for the common goal declined to a large extent. The welfare activities are restricted to individual caste level by forming caste associations. The activities of the panchayat at collective level also came to a standstill. Many people left the old settlement in search of new accommodation. This ultimately resulted in the weakening of the panchayat. Today the panchayat is not performing any function for its members. The association has its existence only because it has got valuable property. Members from a few Manadi communities look after the property of the panchayat. Disputes among the Manadi community members have started for the property.

Analysis

According to Kothari and Maru (1965 : 34) "The concept of caste federation refers to a grouping of a number of endogamous caste groups into a single organisation for common objectives, the realisation of which calls for a pooling of resources or numbers or both". While distinguishing caste federation from caste association they pointed out that "it (caste federation) represents a step beyond caste association in India's development towards a political community". (*ibid* : 35). In the present study it is worth noting that the interest to form this panchayat is not politically motivated, but is to adjust and adapt to the new urban and alien situation. This was formed by a group of lower caste communities who had a common caste status and interest. Among the immigrants there were few upper, middle caste members from Andhra Pradesh. But they were not members of this panchayat. It is not a caste federation in the sense Kothari and Maru proposed. To some extent its activities correspond to a village caste panchayat.

In the early stages of migration the Telugu speaking people in Pune consisted members of the lower caste communities and each of them consisted of only a few members. So each caste group or community was not able to satisfy the socio-cultural needs of its members. Even though few communities had their own caste panchayats, they were not well organised or sufficient enough to meet their members' needs. So communities which had similar interests came together and formed this panchayat. Initially the main function of this panchayat was of adaptive and adjustment type, in order to graft the rural migrants into the city life, providing a socio-cultural environment similar to that of the village. To a great extent this association could meet the primary needs of the members in different ways. For example, it helped the members to arrange their marriage, solving their personal problems, helping them at the time of marriage and funerals, settle all sorts of disputes within and between the community members etc. It also met the socio-religious needs of the members by constructing temples and by celebrating regional festivals.

The association was successful in bringing all the immigrants under one banner who were concentrated mainly in one locality and having similar caste status and interest. By creating an atmosphere conducive for its members to meet and interact in an informal way, the association could achieve in grafting the rural migrants into the city as well as in integrating them to a large extent. To some extent the association was successful in meeting personal as well as family needs of the immigrants. Celebration of religious festivals brought various community members together and enabled to interact informally. Even for celebrating religious festivals and social rituals they were dependent on Telugu immigrant Brahmins. In short this helped them to have minimum contact with the host society during the initial stages of their stay in the city. This also facilitated an atmosphere conducive for them to adapt and adjust to the city life overcoming the cultural shock.

After First World War, the number of immigrants multiplied due to further migration and by birth. By this time most of the early immigrants got well settled in the city. Those who were deprived of good accommodation started moving to different localities in search of the same. A considerable number of Munnurwars selected Rasta Peth as their residential area. Munnurwars represented maximum number among the early immigrants. By 1935, a good number of Munnurwars split off from this panchayat and started their own association, in order to strengthen their community. In a similar way other community members also split off from the panchayat and started their community associations. Due to this Schismogenesis process the panchayat became weak. This shows that during the initial period since the members were few in each community, a need was felt to form an association on a broader multicaste level and when their number increased and they were well settled in the city, the tendency was to form association at individual caste level. This sort of tendency has been reported among the immigrants by many scholars in the Indian urban context (Andrea M. Singh, 1978; Lewandowski, 1981). It is not solely for preserving their ethnic identity that the people come together and form the panchayat, but for their existence in an alien city and to adjust and adapt to an altogether different environment.

Case II

Many Padmasalis from Nizamabad district migrated to Pune in search of job, especially in Handloom industries. They were mainly from the following villages: Kondur, Darpalli, Chirvalgat, Ramadgu and Dubagu. Many of the village immigrants did not have any relatives in Pune and were new to the city. In order to help the people from these villages and Nizamabad district in general, Shri Kurkelli Poshetti formed Padmasali Markhandeya Sangam (Nizamabad Sangam) in 1952. The major aim of this Sangam was to bring the people of their villages together, and get to know them, and try to meet their immediate needs. Membership in this Sangam was exclusively meant for the Padmasalis who had migrated from Nizamabad district.

Activities

For quite some time, from its inception the association was helping the new migrants to find jobs in the city, arranging accommodation and food, especially for those who were helpless. To a certain extent, the Sangam was successful in arranging marriages of the bachelor migrants who did not have their own relatives in Pune. In addition, this association also settled all sorts of disputes among the migrants. Thus the Sangam proved helpful for them. Padmasali migrants who wanted to go back to their native places from Pune faced many problems due to lack of travel facilities. This was the case with the newcomers, also. Trains from Pune reached Nizamabad station in the night. At night, from the station no transport was available to reach their native place. So they had to stay in the station over night. In 1960 they purchased 20 acres of land in Indalbai, Nizamabad district in order to provide accommodation for them. However, they could not fulfil their task immediately. As time passed, migration of Padmasalis slackened and moreover, settled immigrants seldom visit their native place. These days better transport facilities are also available. So they dropped the idea of constructing the Dharmashala there. Now they are thinking of starting a textile industry, so that many of their villagers can find job.

These immigrants residing in Bhavanipeth were getting loans from the Gujarathis and Marwadis at the time of financial crisis. In order to save them from the cruel hands of money lenders, in 1965, they started a Chit Fund. Its facilities are made available to all the members. Whenever they face financial problem they can draw certain amount of money and repay it in instalments with minimal interest. Today, the Chit Fund is functioning nominally and the number of members has reduced.

Present Structure of the Association

This association is managed by 14 committee members and seven office bearers. The office bearers are a president, a vice president, a general secretary, two joint secretaries, an accountant and a cashier. In addition there are five trustees. Out of the five founder trustees, three are still continuing to hold the same posts. Two expired and in their place two new trustees have been nominated.

The main aim of the association was to look after the welfare of new migrants. Most of the early migrants were from villages and city life was new to them. They did not have close relatives in the city. So its major task was to help the new migrants by providing food, accommodation and suitable jobs. Various welfare measures have also been attempted by the association for its members. These activities lost their importance because of the following:

1. The original ethnic enclave got saturated and people started moving to other localities in search of better accommodation. Due to this displacement many people left the association.
2. Recently migration of Padmasalis to Pune in search of jobs in handloom has been lessened thereby dissolving the major objectives of this association. Today its only function is to help the members occasionally by providing loans at the time of financial crisis. No other activities are undertaken by this association, for its members.

Case III

The Padmasali Yuvak Mandal started as an informal gathering of Panchamahal Padmasalis, to meet their community members, and to discuss freely their problems in general. In 1957 they developed it as "Padmasali Yuvak Mandal" with many objectives such as, assisting the immigrants by providing accommodation and finding jobs. This association helps the "Panch Committee" at the time of religious functions. Membership in this association is open for all the Panchamahal Padmasalis.

When the study was carried out there were 125 members, and all of them were from Ganjpeth. Membership fee is Rs. 3 per month. The managing committee consists of 11 members. Out of that five are office bearers consisting of a president, vice-president, secretary, joint secretary and treasurer, and the rest constitute the committee members.

This mandal has rendered various welfare activities for Panchamahal Padmasalis in Pune. When there were large number of new immigrants, the mandal used to arrange accommodation and help them to find jobs in the city. Sometimes, the office of the association was used for accommodating new immigrants at a nominal charge of

Rs. 3 per month. From 1965-68 the mandal conducted tailoring classes for Panchamahal Padmasalis residing in Pune with the help of a tailor master from the community. The classes were arranged free of cost. In 1968 the tailor master left Pune and since the classes have been stopped.

In order to promote education among the students, a nursery was started in Ganjpeth in 1967. Admission to the nursery was given to all community members. As they did not get enough students the nursery was closed in the following year.

Medical facilities at a nominal charge were provided by this association. In 1978 they opened a small dispensary in the office with the help of Dr. A.N. Anmol, who is a member of the community. The doctor could not get enough patients, and therefore, the dispensary was closed in 1979.

This mandal was very active for some time during the early phase of migration and settlement of Padmasalis. In the beginning its major activities were mainly directed towards fresh immigrants. Social welfare activities for the settled immigrants were also undertaken. Today it helps the panch committee at the time of socio-religious functions. Recently this association has started some recreational facilities for its members. Its activities are turning to expressive from instrumental. In effect this association is at present very passive.

Summary

Three associations have been identified as passive and all of them performed instrumental functions. The major functions of these associations were to help the immigrants to adjust and adapt to the city life. To a great extent all the three associations could graft the rural migrants onto the city. Samastha Telugu Manad Panchayat was formed by a group of lower caste communities who migrated in the later decades of colonial period. During that period the members from each community were few. So there was a need to form an association on a broader basis, uniting all the caste groups together. It has helped the migrants to meet their individual needs and the help rendered by a family. It was helpful in meeting their socio-religious needs as well. This association functioned actively for decades. When the immigrants got well adjusted to the city and increased their number, each community split off from this association in order to start their own. So it is clear from this case that fission in the ethnic group is one of the reasons for the passivity of ethnic associations.

Like the earlier Telugu immigrants, Padmasalis were also mainly uneducated and came from villages. The Padmasalis formed three associations primarily for helping the new migrants. They are Jyoti Sangam, Nizamabad Sangam and Padmasali Yuvak Mandal. The migration of Padmasalis from villages for handloom jobs has diminished and hence these three associations have lost their importance. Jyoti Sangam has been disbanded (discussed under the heading Disbanded Association) and the rest two have become passive. Telugu Manad Panchayat and Nizamabad Sangam are likely to be closed down soon, while the chances are that the Padmasali Yuvak Mandal may revive and take up a new form as an youth association.

TRANSFORMED ASSOCIATIONS

Ethnic associations in one way or the other undergo structural and functional modifications during the course of their development. Ethnic associations are resilient and they can attain different forms and content in order to adapt and adjust to the changing situation. In the present study transformed associations have been described as a separate category because this type of associations have reincarnated in different forms, during various stages of their development. Padmasali Yuvak Mandal was formed in 1936 and in due course of time due to external and internal forces it underwent several transformations. Now we will identify the various factors responsible for its transformation and discuss its adaptive potentiality. The phases of transformation of this association is presented in Table 4.4.

Stages of Transformation and Activities

Stage I

In order to help the Padmasali Panch Committee to celebrate various social and religious functions and introduce reforms in the traditional way of functioning of caste panchayats, a group of Padmasali youths came forward and formed Padmasali Yuvak Mandal in 1935. In the following year this association opened a free reading hall, "Padmasali Yuvak Sangh Mofat Vachanalaya". Leaders and educated youths from this community subscribed newspapers for the reading hall. During the Quit India Movement many leaders and educated youths who were active members of this association went to jail, which weakened the association. Simultaneously the reading hall was closed, because nobody was there to subscribe newspapers.

TABLE 4.4: Stages of Transformation, Year of Foundation and Type

Stage	Name of the Association	Year of foundation & transformation	Type
I	Padmasali Yuvak Mandal	1936	Instrumental
II	Padmasali Sudarshan Krida Mandal	1942	Primarily Expressive
III	Samrat Mandal	1944	Primarily Expressive
IV	Padmasali Samrat Mandal	1963	Instrumental Expressive

Stage-II

After a lapse of three years i.e. in 1944, the youths of this community reformed this association as "Padmasali Sudarshan Krida Mandal". The objective of this mandal was to give training to the youths in regional and local sports and games. At the same time it retained the objective of "Padmasali Yuvak Mandal" i.e. to help the Panch Committee at the time of social and religious functions. However, its major effort was directed towards arranging sports and games. In addition to sports and games this association gave special training to its members in the regional dance form known as "tippiri". Coaching was arranged in games like *kabbadi* and *attepattya*. The mandal reopened the reading hall and gave it a new name, "Padmasali Sudarshan Mofat Vachanalaya". The life span of this association was only two years. After two years this association further transformed and re-established itself as Samrat Mandal.

Stage III

As a minority, Padmasali community was treated by the locals as "foreigners". They had to face discrimination and harassment from the receiving society. The locals used to call them derogatively as "Kamathis". In order to have friendly relations with the locals, the Padmasali Sudarshan Krida Mandal was renamed as Samrat Mandal.

They encourage the locals to take membership in this association. Even though they gave membership to the locals, the main objectives of this association remained basically same as that of the Padmasali Sudarshan Krida Mandal. But, the Samrat Mandal stopped arranging the regional games. Instead importance was given to the local games and sports. From 1947 to 1960, this association had good teams in "kabbadi" and "attepattya" which are famous games in Maharashtra. The team won the "attepattya" championship at the Pune District level competitions on several occasions. In 1950 this mandal organised "attepattya" tournaments at the Maharashtra state level. An in that tournament the then vice-president of India N. Sanjeeva Reddy, distributed the prizes. In short this association helped the Padmasalis to demonstrate their ability in local games and sports and prove to the locals that they are not merely workers or "kamathis".

In addition to helping the Padmasali Panch Committee to organise regional religious festivals the Samrat Mandal, celebrated several local religious functions, especially the Ganesh festival, jointly with the local population. The removal of the name "Padmasali" from this association and the new name "Samrat Mandal" broadened the base and this attracted many locals to this association. The participation of the local population in the activities of the association lead to better relations between the immigrants and the locals.

Stage IV

The association did not have an office of its own until 1963. In the year 1963 the Panch Committee was approached by the association for an office. The Panch Committee agreed to give a room to the association on a condition that the association should be renamed as "Padmasali Samrat Mandal". The Committee also insisted that the membership in this association should restricted to the Padmasalis. By this time the population of Padmasalis was comparatively large in Bhavanipeth, and therefore they could restrict the membership of this association to Padmasali youths. So on 1st August, 1963, they removed the names of all other community members except the Padmasalis from the membership list and renamed this association as "Padmasali Samrat Mandal". Since then the membership is restricted to the Telugu Youths. With this change in name and membership, its activities also changed. The importance of sports and games reduced, and the emphasis shifted to social welfare activities for the Padmasalis residing in Pune.

In 1964 the association opened a medical aid centre and adult education centre for the Padmasalis. This was inaugurated by the then Mayor of Pune. A well wisher from the community donated almost all the equipments and instruments to start the medical aid centre. This medical aid centre was open to Padmasali community members, at a nominal charge. Nearly 1,000 people from the community took advantages of these medical facilities during 1964. The adult education centre helped 82 members from this community to pass the marathi examination conducted by the municipal education board.

Even though its membership was restricted to the Padmasalis, the association did not restrict its welfare activities to their own community. Certain facilities are open for all other community members residing in the locality. People from Bhavanipeth and adjoining areas did participate in the celebration of Ganesh festival organised by the Padmasali Samrat Mandal irrespective of their caste and creed. For the decoration of Ganesh and for the celebration of the festival peacefully, Padmasali Samrat Mandal got special certificates from the Mayor of Pune in 1979 and 1980. In 1981 they were awarded silver shields and a cup by the Pune Municipal Corporation. The association celebrate *Dahihandi*, *Desara* and *Makarashankranthi* festivals every year with great enthusiasm. By celebrating these local religious festivals and by inviting various other community members, to take part in it, this association has been attempting to integrate different ethnic groups residing in Bhavanipeth.

On 1st August, 1964, Padmasali Samrat Mandal reopened the reading hall and left it for the youths of Bhavanipeth irrespective of their community backgrounds. Seven daily newspapers in Hindi and Marathi and one weekly are being subscribed by this association.

Every year the mandal celebrate national days like Independence Day and Republic Day. On Republic Day they have been arranging sports and games for the residents of Bhavanipeth. The competitions arranged on the Republic Day include 100 meter race, "rangoli", slow cycling and music competition. Slow cycling is meant for elders and the rest of the games and competitions are meant for children.

Summary

The association was started in order to help the Panch Committee to celebrate various functions and to persuade them to make changes in the traditional mode of functioning of the caste panchayat. It was active for a span of three years and then became weak, because most of the active members left the association. After a lapse of three years, the youth from the community gave a new life to this association. When it was revived its function was primarily expressive. They gave training to the members in local as well as regional games and sports. It was active only for two years. In order to have peaceful and friendly relations with the locals the association opened its membership to the local community youths. To attract them they emphasised the local games and sports. At a later stage when Padmasalis increased in number in the ethnic locality, they restricted membership to Padmasalis, and changed its function from instrumental to instrumental expressive. Subsequently, the association became very active and started various welfare measures for the community members. However, the facilities of this association were also made available for the other communities residing in the ethnic neighbourhood. This helped to integrate the people residing in Bhavanipeth with the immigrants.

The case study presented above suggests that ethnic association tend to be very resilient. In order to adjust and adapt to the changing situation this association underwent several transformations.

DISBANDED ASSOCIATIONS

Six associations have been identified as disbanded and all of them were instrumental in their functions, except one which was expressive. Except one all of them were formed before the onset of industriali-azation of Pune. They flourished in different time periods and at various stages of the development of the Telugu speaking immigrant communities in Pune. All the associations which are identified as disbanded had large life spans. Table 4.5 shows the associations which are disbanded along with the year of foundation and the year when they were disbanded. They are classified on the basis of their functions, and arranged communitywise.

Case I

During the end of 19th century and the beginning of 20th century majority of Telugu immigrants were uneducated and facilities for educating their children were scarce in the city of Pune. Many attempts were made by Telugu leaders to impart education among the Telugu immigrants of Pune.

In 1903, prominent leaders and social workers from this community started the telugu education fund in order to institute and to give scholarships and financial assistance to the needy and deserving Telugu students.

TABLE 4.5: Disbanded Associations along with the year of Foundation, Year of disbandments and type

Case	Name of the Association	Year of foundation	Year of disbandment	Type
1.	Telugu Education Fund	1903	1945	Instrumental
2.	Telugu General Library	1903	1950	Instrumental
3.	Jyothi Sangam	1957	1970	Instrumental
4.	Markhandeya Mela	1937	1947	Instrumental
5.	Tippiri Mela	1930	1950	Expressive
6.	Telugu Madelwar Yuvak Mandal	1934	1945	Instrumental

One of the important personages who took active part in forming the education fund was Advocate Polas Rajanna Lingu. He was the first president of the fund and he continued in this post till his death. Both the library and education fund was started in Pune Camp, where the community members concentrated. Facilities of the education fund and library were open for all the Telugu speakers irrespective of their caste, creed or religion. Many Telugu students belonging to different strata took the benefit of this fund. This was functioning till 1940's. At this stage those who were managing the fund lost interest, in the Telugu education fund as it was meant for the Telugu students in general. Their attention turned to providing educational facilities to their own sub-groups. So the sub-groups started providing scholarships and other help to own community students, thus weakening the Telugu education fund. Today most of the communities under study provide scholarships and other incentives to their own community members. In this way by 1940's it became dysfunctional.

Case II

Like the Telugu education fund, the Telugu library was also founded for the welfare of the Telugu speaking people in Pune. Educated people from the community contributed money and supplied books for the library. But it functioned only for a few years. A split among the Telugu community weakend this association. After the Telugu library was disbanded, a few youths from the Munnarwar community came forward to give a new life to this neglected library. They collected books from Telugu general library and a well wisher from the community presented enough books to start a new library. Another well wisher, gifted a room in Rashta Peth. Thus on 11th October, 1921 on Vijaya Dashmi day the Telugu General library became Telugu Munnurwar library and reading room. For 14 years i.e. from 1935 to 1949 the library was getting financial backing from the Pune Municipality. When the major source of income stopped, they decided to collect funds from the members. Membership in this library was given only to Telugu speaking people till 1940. After 1940, membership was given to other community members on certain conditions. Inspite of opening the memberships to others, during 1945 there were only 34 members. Most of them were from Munnurwar community. The total number of books in the library were 550 , of which 295 were in Marathi, 200 were in English and 50 were in Telugu. Three dailies, three weeklies and four magazines were also subscribed by this library. This library functioned till 1950, and later on, no one took active interest to run this library, thus 1950 the library was closed down.

Case III

Two associations have been identified among the Padmasalis which were helpful in grafting the rural migrants to the city, especially during the initial stage of migration. They were Jyothi Sangam and Nizamabad Sangam. When the migration of the community members to Pune slackened the first one disbanded and the functional status of the other became passive.

Jyothi Sangam was started in 1957 by Mr. Mallayya Chinnappa Mitthapalli, Dr. P. Ananthan and V.R. Gurrum with a view of helping the Padmasali migrants to Pune from Korutla village in Andhra Pradesh. The major aim of this association was to bring them together, so that they would get to know each other, help each other in finding out jobs, arrange accommodation, food and try to solve their personal as well as family problems. Membership in this particular association was restricted to Padmasalis who had migrated from Korutla village in particular and the migrants from Karimnagar district in general. At the time of foundation of this association its name was "Korutla Padmasali Samudhu Jyoti Sangam". At a later stage i.e. after a few months of its inception, the name of this association was changed into "Padmasali Jyoti Sangam" and opened its membership to all the Telugu speaking Padmasalis in Pune. But in practice only migrants from Korutla village were members of this association. Initially there were 50 members, and the membership fee was two annas per month. By 1960, the total number of members increased to 150.

Activities

For quite some time, this association helped the new migrants in finding accommodation, food and jobs, and assisted bachelor migrants in arranging their marriages. It provided medical facilities to the sick and supported them during their sickness. It also took active part in educating the migrants and their children. Prime importance was given to teaching Telugu which is their mother tongue. Efforts were also made to teach Hindi, Marathi and English, so that they would be able to read and improve their general knowledge. Classes were conducted by experts in these languages. Admission was open for all the Telugu Padmasalis and no fee was charged from them. Classes were conducted late in the evening, so that all the working people could attend the classes. In the beginning nearly 60 to 70 members including youths as well as older members used to attend the classes. After the course they conducted examinations by inviting experts from "Andhra Saraswathy Parishad" which is a private institute in Hyderabad. This institute gave certificates to the deserving students. This certificate is useful in getting teaching posts in schools especially in Andhra Pradesh. Examinations in Telugu language were conducted for the following course, viz. "Prathamik", "Madhyamik", "Praveshika", and "Visharadi". Due to the efforts of the association 30 students passed the Prathamik Examination and 10 passed Madhyamik.

Till 1962 the association conducted classes in Telugu with great enthusiasm. Later on the members did not show any interest in studying their mother tongue as many Padmasalis felt that studying Telugu will not help them in any way. Most of them were already settled in Pune. By 1962 the scheme was discontinued. This organization also arranged Telugu Dramas by inviting drama troops from Andhra Pradesh.

In order to impress upon the immigrants the importance of Telugu language and culture, the association brought scholars in Telugu literature and arranged important lecture series. In 1958-59 a "Kavi Sammelan" was organized by the association. They brought Kappa Ganthalu Laxmana Shastri from Hyderabad, who was a famous poet in Telugu language. He stressed the importance of one's own mother tongue and also talked about the greatness and sweetness of Telugu language and advised the people not to forget their own language and cultural heritage.

Present Status of the Association

The association helped to organize and unite all the migrants of Korutla village under one banner. This unity helped them to get their representatives elected into the Pune Municipality. In the due course their identity based on their village of origin has undergone change. By 1970's most of the villagers have aligned themselves to various national or regional political parties, and the unity on the basis of village has been lost. Moreover, now the influx of new migrants to Pune was lessened and those who migrated earlier are well settled and established in the city. So the functions rendered by this association during the initial period of migration are no more relevant now. Subsequently this association has now been disbanded.

Case IV

During the Colonial rule in India, public meetings aimed at motivating patriotic feeling among the masses were banned. So Bal Gangadhar Tilak advised the people to start religious procession at the time of Ganesh Festival in order to bring people together and to create social awareness and patriotic feelings among them. During the season, religious processions and meetings usually turned into political rallies. Most of the patriotic ideas were communicated through songs and poems. These poems and songs depicted the injustices of the British and atrocities committed by them in different parts of India. Padmasali Markhandeya *Mela* was an informal association started for this purpose by the Padmasalis. This association was started in the name of their "Kula Devi" Markhandeya in the month of August, 1937. The aim of this *Mela* was to motivate and inspire patriotic feelings among their community members in particular and the Maharashtrians in general.

During the Ganesh festival the 'mela' used to arrange procession and public meetings from the day of installation of Ganesh idol till the immersion day. The programme began usually with the worship of their Goddess Markhandeya. They used to sing religious and patriotic songs in Telugu wherever their community members are concentrated. They gave public speeches in Telugu to make their community members aware of their socio-political conditions. Through speeches, they requested their community members to abstain from drinks, stop child marriages, and stress the importance and necessity of education among them.

During the Holi festival this association used to arrange dramas in Telugu and Marathi. The themes of the dramas were often nationalism and social reform. They had staged "Bhaktha druv", "Kacha Devayani" etc. This 'mela' was functioning from 1937 till the Independence of India. When India become independent the association ceased to function and eventually got disbanded from the scene.

Case V

Tippri Mela was started in the year 1930 to encourage Tippiri a folk dance which is very popular in Andhra Pradesh. Tippiri dances were organized in the month of February. The tippiri is a stick with a thick base and a tapering end. Pieces of long cloth are attached to the pole on a suspended disc. The strips of cloths are held by the dances in their hands, normally eight to ten pairs of dancers participate in the dance. Keeping tune with music they dance and weave various patterns with the help of the strip pieces. During the initial stages of their migration this dance was zealously performed every year by the Padmasalis. As this dance is not popular in Maharashtra, the descendants of the first generation immigrants do not show any interest in this dance. They are more interested in local dances and festivals. So around 1950 this dance disappeared from the community and consequently the association disbanded.

Case VI

A group of youths from Telugu Madelwar community at Camp area came forward and formed a mandal in 1936. The intention of this mandal was to help the community members at the time of marriage and funerals. During this period the Telugu Madelwar caste panchayat was managed by illiterate and old members. They did not manage the caste panchayat in a systematic way. They used to spend the community income for parties and drinks. The prime aim of this association was to dissuade the old members to change the traditional method of conducting the caste panchayat and demand reforms within the panchayat. For some time this mandal helped the panchayat to organize and celebrate various functions and festivals. They also collected the membership fee and marriage cess "Katnum" regularly. They used this amount for buying cooking utensils and other equipment for the panchayat.

The Mandal served the panchayat till 1950. By this time this panchayat had a few educated members and the need for a separate association became irrelevant. So in 1950 the association disappeared from the scene.

Analysis

The early Telugu migrants to Pune belonged to various communities and the members from each community were few. Their initial settlement was in Camp. The first two associations viz. Telugu education fund and Telugu library were formed by them. The facilities of these two associations were open for all the Telugu immigrants in Pune. Most of the Telugu migrants in Pune utilized the facilities of these two associations. When the members of each community increased in number, each community started strengthening their own group by forming various welfare associations. Initially all these communities were functioning as a single ethnic group based on the linguistic identity. With the fission of the ethnic group into caste based sub-groups, the importance of common interest association become insignificant. It is due to the change in ethnic identity, the first two associations were dissolved.

Case III shows that just the opposite process of fission i.e. fusion of the sub-groups lead to its disbandment. This association was formed by a group of migrants from a particular village and its activities were restricted to that particular group. Its main function was to help the villagers especially the newcomers to adapt and adjust to the city life. Initially all the migrants from the village settled in one locality. When the migration of the villagers ceased and the migrants got well adjusted to the city life, the association became less important. Ultimately the identity on the basis of village, kinship and friendship transformed itself to caste and political level. This shifting of identity from a village level to the caste and political level lead to the disbandment of this association.

Case IV shows that, the association stopped functioning after its major aim was achieved. The association could awaken the members politically and generate in them patriotism and a desire to fight against the foreign rule in India. When India became independent its major aim was fulfilled, and simultaneously the Association disbanded.

So far we have seen that fission, fusion, and socio-political changes lead to the disbandment of ethnic associations. There is yet another factor which leads to the disbandment of ethnic associations. The first generation migrants take active part in promoting their regional cultural activities. While the subsequent generations appears to loose interest in their past traditions. They tend to adopt the local cultural and social traditions to some extent. The process of deculturation of the second generation also lead to the disbandment of the ethnic associations.

The ethnic associations tend to disband once their intended function has been fulfilled. Case V strengthened this conclusion. This case shows that a factional grouping within an ethnic group lead to the formation of associations. Its main aim was to demand radical change and reform in the traditional mode of functioning of the caste panchayat. When they got some representation in the panchayat, there was no need for a separate association and therefore this association got disbanded.

Out of the six associations under discussion five were instrumental in function. Only one association was identified as expressive type which was aimed at promoting their regional culture. Almost all the associations could satisfy their intended functions to a certain extent. An interplay of various internal and external factors like fission, fusion of ethnic groups social and political change, deculturation and attainment of intended functions lead to the disbandment of ethnic associations. Often the stage prior to disbandment is one of passivity. From the analysis it is clear that the reasons for passivity as well as disbandment are related to some extent.

Conclusion

This Chapter deals with the changing role of ethnic associations over time. Based on the structural and functional adaptations, we have proposed four stages of development of ethnic associations. They are active, passive, transformed and disbanded. Ethnic associations are formed by the immigrants in the city to attain certain goals. They are active for some time when the need exists. However, it is found that due to various external and internal factors, some of the associations became passive and transformed, and others disappeared from the scene.

A large number of associations have been identified as active. They include associations which were formed during the initial stages of migration and later. One of the characteristics of active association is that they have specialised in functions, except the Andhra Association which was formed by the recent immigrants. The functions rendered by active associations were mainly integrative and welfare oriented. Youth, religious and community welfare associations were found to be good integrative mechanisms. This was achieved by giving membership and extending facilities of the ethnic associations to other community members. Three associations have been identified as passive. All these associations were directed to the welfare of the new immigrants to the city. These associations became passive because of fission in the ethnic group and attainment of their intended functions. Transformed associations were very resilient and they showed that ethnic associations can change form and content in order to adapt to the changing situations. The transformation of ethnic associations are co-related mainly with the integrative functions. The integrative functions helped the migrants to have friendly relations with the receiving society whereby avoiding conflict. Six associations have been identified as disbanded. This is due to fission, fusion, deculturation, attainment of intended functions and socio-political change in the ethnic community. Out of the six associations which were classified under this head, two could achieve their intended functions fully before they were disbanded.

All the four types of associations have had large life spans and they were stable through time. Even the disbanded associations showed remarkable longivity. Almost all the associations could achieve their intended functions to a great extent. The formation, preservation, fission, fusion, passivity, transformation and disbandment of ethnic associations reflect the changing needs of the immigrant community under study. The associations which were formed by the immigrants during the initial stages of their migration vary from those formed in later years in their structure and function. The associations which were formed during the initial stages were adaptive and adjustment in functions. These associations played a major role in cushioning the cultural shock, which the immigrants faced during the initial stages of their stay in the city. All the disbanded associations were instrumental in their functions except one which was expressive. Similarly all the passive associations were instrumental in their function. The transformed associations were initially instrumental and later on developed into instrumental-expressive. An inter-play of instrumental and expressive functions are the characteristic feature of active associations.

The functions of ethnic associations undergo changes over time. During later stage of the migration and settlement the adjustment and adaptive functions change into integrative and welfare functions. The importance of primary associations are not decreasing nor are they turning into purely expressive associations as Sheldon (1976) and others have proposed. A combination of both expressive, and instrumental associations are active among the ethnic groups under study. In a city like Pune which is fast changing into an industrial complex one may expect a combination of both the types of associations rather than purely expressive ones.

A sequential development of ethnic associations as proposed by Price (1975) is not applicable to all contexts. In this study we found that different types of associations were formed by the immigrants during various stages of their stay in the city. The variability in structure and function of these associations may be accounted for the structure of the immigrants population and the process of urbanization.

Ethnic associations make significant contribution to the preservation of ethnic identity of the immigrant community by simulating the culture of the immigrants' place of origin. From the analysis it is clear that various modalities are adopted by ethnic associations to promote immigrants' culture in a distant city.

5

ETHNIC ASSOCIATIONS AND BACKWARD CLASS MOVEMENT: A Case Study of Padmasali Sabha

The hierarchical stratification of Indian society on the basis of caste has adversely affected the upward mobility of lower caste members. In pre-British India, the lower caste communities were deprived of religious, economic and educational equalities. The inequalities in all these fields were said to be divinely sanctioned. Yet, several attempts were made by the lower caste members to raise their status in the social system. However, upper caste members stood as a barrier against their upward social mobility. With the establishment of a democratic system of law and order, the stated goals of equality gave a new impetus to the movement of the backward classes in India.

In India the backward classes' movement has passed through various stages and each stage has been characterized by different aims and objectives. During the medieval period, i.e. before the advent of the British regime, the caste system was so rigid that mobility within it was very difficult. Sanskritisation was the only means for their upward social mobility. However, by this means they could only adopt the religious customs, practices and style of life of the twice born.

The establishment of British rule in India gave a new stimulus to the backward classes movement. The introduction of new means of communication, postal system and modern education, etc. helped the caste members to have wider spatial mobility, which in turn helped them to organise themselves at a wider level on the basis of caste.

"As the internal bonds of solidarity were extended over wider areas, regional associations were established by aspirant castes with the avowed purpose of elevating the status and prestige of the community as a whole, by standardising the 'purifying' customs in the process of Sanskritisation. These associations sought to organize and unite all members of the caste so that their claims might be advanced more effectively against other castes" (Hardgrave, 1968:10). The emergence of caste based ethnic associations, or caste-sabhas, came handy to these castes as means to fight for their rights and demands which had been hitherto denied to them. The role of caste-sabhas in demanding higher status through Sanskritisation was very obvious when the first census was taken in 1901. The leaders of various caste-sabhas demanded that the census authorities should place their castes at the level of a higher varna. This claim for the twice born status of high rank was substantiated in terms of mythical stories about the origin of caste and by other means. Srinivas (1972: 98-99) gave an extract from the census of 1931 of the United Provinces where 148 of the so called lower castes claimed higher status. Out of the 175 claims made by the 148 castes, 39 were made through caste-sabhas. Rao (1978:197) interpreted the claims for status in a high varna as ". . . .not a process of imitation but a language of aggression by which sections of the Backward Classes challenged the monopoly of the upper caste in terms of access to the rituals and religious services of Brahmanical Hinduism from which they had been barred for centuries".

The emergence of caste-sabhas gave new life to the backward classes movement by strengthening their group solidarity and identity. For quite some time, i.e. till Independence, caste-sabhas were mainly used as a means for upward social mobility through Sanskritisation. However, through Sanskritisation they could achieve only positional rather than structural change. When India became Independent, various Constitutional guarantees were given to the backward classes communities in the areas of education, jobs, administration and politics. In order to avail themselves of the benefits, the caste sabhas took a reverse turn, i.e. "desanskritisation". In recent years, the stranglehold of caste sabhas has increased considerably. Those castes having a similar occupation ad sharing the same tradition and status have tried to come together even cutting across linguistic boundaries to press their claims and demand the constitutional benefits.

Many studies have shown that the initial concern of caste-sabhas was to reform caste customs, later changed to economic, political and social welfare activities. A few studies showing this tendency are referred here. Rudolph and Rudolph (1960) have shown that the Vanniars had claimed the status of Kshatriya as early as 1871. After Independence they organized themselves under the Tamil Nadu Toiler Party, and wanted to be considered as a backward caste and demanded seats to be reserved for them in legislative assembly and government services. Another study indicating this tendency has been conducted by Hardgrave (1968) on the Nadars of Tamil Nadu. In the 1891 census, the Nadars (the toddy tapers) were classed among untouchables, and were not allowed to use the wells of the higher castes or to enter the temples. In 1910 a representation was made through the Nadar Mahajana Sangam, in order to register Nadars as Kshatriyas by presenting historical evidences to support this. In 1930, and also later in 1940, the Nadar Mahajana Sangam requested the government to list the Nadars among the educationally backward communities so that educational concessions might be available to the Nadar students. After Independence and the establishment of the backward classes commission, Nadars made a concerted effort to have themselves listed as depressed class.

The Government of India had appointed two Commissions to identify the socially and educationally backward classes in India. The first Commission was appointed in 1953 under the Chairmanship of Shri Kaka Kalekar and the second in 1977 under the Chairmanship of Shri B.P. Mandal. During the time of the appointment of the Backward Classes Commission, many middle castes and other backward communities, through political leaders and through their associations pressurised the Commission to include their respective communities in the socially and educationally backward classes, so as to get the benefits meant for the backward classes. Even castes belonging to backward classes pressed their demands to place them in order to get more benefits. On this tendency, the Mandal Commission reports: ". . . .a large number of public men and caste associations argued their case for the inclusion of a particular caste in the list of other Backward Classes. Some of them, whose caste was already notified as backward by the State concerned, wanted it to be included in the list of Scheduled Castes or Scheduled Tribes. Nearly 3/4 of the respondents appearing before the Commission belonged to this category" (Report of the Backward Classes Commission , Vols. I and II, Chapter X, 1980:46).

The present Chapter attempts to analyse the changing role of Caste Sabha with special reference to backward classes movement. In this Chapter we intend to discuss the development of Padmasali caste sabhas from a historical perspective, focussing our attention on the change that had taken place in their functions, organizational set up, objectives, and leadership pattern. The Padmasalis are weavers by trade and the community is distributed mainly in Andhra Pradesh,

Gujarat, Maharashtra, Karnataka, Madhya Pradesh, Tamil Nadu and Kerala. According to the Constitution of Padmasali Mahasabha adopted on 10th July, 1982 the approximate population distribution on the basis of State/Region is given in Table 5.1.

TABLE 5.1: Distribution of Padmasalis on the basis of state/region

Sl. No.	State/Region	Population (Lakh)
1.	Kerala (State)	1
2.	Tamil Nadu (State)	5
3.	Circars (Regional)	10
4.	Rayalseema (Regional)	5
5.	Telengana (Regional)	10
6.	Karnataka (State)	3
7.	Western Maharashtra (Regional)	2.5
8.	Marathwada (Regional)	0.5
9.	Vidarbha (Regional)	1.0
10.	Greater Bombay (Regional)	1.5
11.	Gujarat (State)	0.25
12.	Madhya Pradesh (State)	0.5
13.	Orissa (State)	1.0
	Total	41.25

Mythology and Aspiration of Padmasalis

"Sale" is a general term applied to a group of caste among the Telugus who have adopted weaving as their occupation. It comes from the word "Salika" which is of Sanskrit origin and which means "weaver". In Andhra Pradesh there are three endogamous groups among the sales. They are Padmasali, Pattusale and Sakunsale. The origin of these endogamous groups is not clear. However, all of them have a common belief, concerning their descent from Markhandeya, the God's weaver. Bhavanarishi is believed to be the man who invented weaving. Among the sales, Padmasali is the most important division. Pattusale corrupted into "Padisale", the people who weave silk cloths. Most of them have become Lingayats. The Sakunsalis seems to have come from North India, and the meaning of the term is not known.

Among the Padmasalis, there were two main groups—the Orthodox Hindus and the Lingayats. Besides the division into Lingayat and Hindus, the Padmasali caste was further divided into a number of exogamous divisions. These divisions were denoted by family names, which were associated with the name of some "rishis". There were 101 such different families, some bearing names of familiar objects, but it was difficult to find out the significance of their family names (Iyyer, 1931: 561-562). Some of the anonymous sections of the Padmasalis bore the name of Brahmanical "gotras". But in the regulation of their marriages, the Padmasalis followed the family names and the authority of "gotras" was practically disregarded. It was also found that many illiterate numbers of the caste were utterly ignorant of the existence of the gotras (Syed Husan, 1920:538).

The demands of Padmasalis for high social status were followed by various mythical stories of their high origin and their relation of god. Like other lower castes, Padmasalis also support their high Sanskrit origin with various myths and legendary stories. One such a version is given below. In order to cloth the nakedness of human beings Lord Siva commissioned Markhandeya to perform a sacrifice and Bhavanarishi came out of the holy fire, holding a lotus flower (padma) in his hand. He married two women, Prasannavati and Badravati, daughters of Surya (the Sun), and had a hundred and one sons, all of them took to weaving cloth out of the fibre of the lotus flower. They became the progenitors of the one hundred and one "gotras" of this caste. Lord Surya, being pleased with what they did, gave them a fifth Veda called *Padma Veda*, and so men of this caste belong to "Padmasakha" and "Markhandeya Sutra", analogous to the "Sakhas", "Sutras" and gotras of the Brahmins. They profess to have followed rites prescribed for Brahmans, till the beginning of the Kali age. One of their craftsmen, named Padmaksha declined to reveal the virtues of a miraculous gem which "Brahma" had given to their caste, to "Ganapati", who sought to learn the secret which they had been entrusted to keep, and who, on his wish not being gratified, cursed them to a lower status. It is said, that one "Parabrahmamurti", otherwise known as Padmabhavacharya, redistributed the castes into ninety-six "gotras" arranged them in eight groups and established four mathas with a guru for each group (Iyyer, 1931: 559-60). Such versions pertaining to their high Sanskritic origin became popular especially with the advent of the first census enumeration.

The guru of the Padmasalis is Tata Acharya, one of the hereditary chiefs of the Vaishnava Brahmin. He lived at Doda Bala Pura and bestows "updesa" and "chakrantikam" (Buchanan, 1807:225). He had a deputy by name Pattabhai Ramaswamy who attended births, marriages, and burials of the Padmasalis, wherever, they were concentrated. The guru of Padmasalis and his deputy played an important role in raising the social and religious status of the Padmasalis. They travelled intensively and advised the Padmasalis to abstain from non-vegetarian food, alcholism and widow re-marriage and advocated them to wear the sacred thread. They also proposed many Brahmanical rites in order to raise their social status.

The Padmasalis are widely scattered and the degree of ceremonial purity of their customs varies in different regions. In Telugu region all Brahmanical rites were reported to be strictly observed. In the district of Medak of Hyderabad State, all sorts of religious ceremonies were performed by the Padmasalis, instead of the Brahmins. The Padmasalis tried to abstain from flesh and liquor, looked upon widow re-marriage as a degraded act and began wearing the scared thread. This innovation was said to have been brought about by their guru and his deputy. The innovation of wearing the sacred thread was done in Sholapur and Pune by Shri Pattabhi Ramaswamy in the later years of the 19th century. The thread wearing ceremony has been an important life cycle ceremony among the community members. However, now-a-days its importance has declined. In Pune 10 to 15 per cent of the Padmasalis still wear the sacred thread during the festival of Markhandeya on the day of "Naralipoornima". Even though many people do not wear the sacred thread, according to the community rule, they should wear it during their marriage ceremony. From the historical survey it is clear that Sanskritisation played a major role in raising the caste status till recently. However, the aspiration for twice born caste status among the Padmasalis is now on a decline.

Despite the decline in the process of Sanskritisation, the aspiration for the twice born status is still very much alive. The community members are trained in Brahmanical rites with the help of learned Brahmins scholars and the Padmasalis have several "vedic schools" in different parts of the country. The following description substantiates this trend.

In Sholapur and Pune, till the later decades of the 19th century, all sorts of religious ceremonies of the Padmasalis were conducted by the Brahmins. However, at present Padmasalis trained in Brahmanical rites perform the religious ceremonies in the community. Around 1930, eight youths were trained to perform the Brahmanical rites in Sholapur. Two well known Sanskrit scholars, Vedashiromani Battiproal Bapannayya and Kantha Varupu Vardayya Shastri from Guntur district, were invited by the Padmasali community to train the youths in Brahmanical rites. These scholars stayed in Sholapur for four months and gave intensive training to their disciples.

With the help of the community leaders, the Padmasali priests started the "Padmasali Purohit Sangh" in 1934 at Sholapur. This association has been registered under the Public Trust Act. The major aim of this association is to give training to Padmasalis in religious ceremonies and help the community members to perform religious rituals. Padmasalis from different parts of the country are being trained by this association. At present there are 56 Padmasalis undergoing training in Brahmanical rites. After the completion of the training the Institute conducts an examination, "Purohit Sangh Examination", and distributes certificates to successful candidates. This association is constructing a new building in order to provide better facilities to the trainees. It has a good collection of vedic books in Telugu, Marathi and Hindi. Following the Padmasalis in Sholapur, the Ahmednagar Padmasalis also have started an association on similar lines. One of the priests from Sholapur informed me that the only difference in rituals performed by the Brahmins and the Padmasalis is that a Brahmin follows "Puranokth" whereas the Padmasali follows "Vedokth".

Out of the eight Padmasalis who got intensive training from the Brahmin scholars, two came to Pune around 1940 and trained the Padmasalis in Pune. They stayed for six months in Pune and taught *Yajurveda*, "Yakshayagadi" and Brahmanical rituals. Apart from this, in 1946, Sreeram Buchayya and two of his friends went to Gurukul Kangadi in Haridwar and studied in Haridwar seven years. After returning from Haridwar they taught these "mantras" and "purohit karmas" to few of their community members in Pune. Today in Pune all the religious ceremonies are being performed by the Padmasali "Purohits". Occasionally other ethnic groups like Gujaratis, Marwadis, Punjabis and Marathas invite Padmasali priests for conducting their religious ceremonies. Padmasali priests are invited generally for performing naming ceremony, house warming ceremony, and "Satyanarayana Pooja".

In addition to training Padmasalis to conduct the religious rituals, the ethnic associations of Padmasalis in Pune have been identified in promoting and reinforcing religious identity. These associations strive to inculcate good habits among the Padmasalis by following the principles and ideals of Hindu saints. There are two such associations in Pune. They are: (1) Yogeshwar Swadhyaya Kendra, and (2) Vaidik

Satsang Mandal. Inspired by the "Pravachans" of the Maharashtrian Saint Parampujya Panduranga Shastri Athavale, Late Sri Sambayya Narasayya Dasri formed the Yogeshwar Swadhyaya Kendra in 1960. The aim of this association is to spread the principles of Gita among the community members. The association requests the people not to be selfish, abstain from drinks and smoking, to behave well and look after their parents. From 9.00 a.m. to 10.00 a.m. on Sundays this association arranges "bhajans" and "Gita Parayan". They arrange group discussions on Thursday on various religious topics. The people who attend these functions are mainly the youth.

Vaidik Satsang Mandal is also working on the same line as that of Yogeshwar Swadhyaya Kendra. This Mandal was started in 1964 with the intention of providing religious facilities to the migrants and to persuade them to give up their bad habits. This association also conducts "bhajans", "havans", "homs" and "pravachans".

The brief description of the two religious associations of Padmasalis in Pune shows that the aspiration of Padmasalis for the status of the twice born castes started more than a century ago. Their efforts on this line for upward mobility continue to this days. However, after Independence the process of Sanskritisation has lost its momentum. Instead, their reference groups became backward classes, in order to gain access to the privileges and advantages offered through the protective discrimination, of the Scheduled Caste, Scheduled Tribes and Backward Classes. What follows is a detailed case study of one of the major caste sabhas of the Padmasalis. This case study is presented in order to show the course of events, which turned the attention of the community from Sanskritisation to Backward Class movement.

All India Padmasali Mahasabha: Historical Perspective

Phase

The Padmasalis staying in urban areas started their communal activities with the advent of the 20th century, initially forming Markhandeya Samaj at Hyderabad. This Samaj used to arrange weekly bhajans and celebration of yearly festivals. Later on the Padmasalis from Secunderabad also joined them, which helped to strengthen their group activities. Later on in 1913 this association developed into a state wide Mahasabha known as Nizam Rashtra Padmasali Mahasabha with the objective of reforming the caste customs on the lines of those of the twice born castes and to improve the socio-economic conditions of the Padmasali caste members throughout the State. From 1913 to 1918 this Sabha held six conferences in various part of the Nizam state. During the span of six years, the Sabha had passed various resolutions in order to end the diversities in the caste customs. During the third conference a resolution was passed in order to prepare a constitution of the Mahasabha. Accordingly a committee was appointed and the Committee prepared a Constitution which the Sabha accepted. The main objectives of the Mahasabha were as follows:

(i) to end the diversities in customs among the Padmasalis at different places;
(ii) to end the illiteracy among the members of the community;
(iii) to put an end to the social evils in the community and to improve the caste customs;
(iv) to developed handloom occupation which is their main occupation;
(v) to improve the economic status of the caste;
(vi) to acquire securities and rights from the government;
(vii) to unite the Padmasalis who migrated to other states, with those in the home state; and,
(viii) to make efforts towards the all round development of the community.

Phase II

The sixth Padmasali Mahasabha of the State of Nizam was held at Cuddapah, which was presided over by Sri Nukal Venkat Subayya. He was a wealthy businessman from the community and had good influence over the people especially in Cuddapah district. After the sixth conference of the Padmasalis in the State of Nizam, he hold an All India Conference of Padmasalis, and brought together all Padmasalis who were scattered in different parts of the country. He was assisted in this task by Sri Karyampudi Venkatakavi Shatavadhani. Sri Venkata Kavi Shatavadani was a highly educated person and a poet who had dedicated his life for the development of the Padmasalis. Thanks to the untiring work of the caste leaders the first All India Padmasali Mahasabha was held at Pullempeth in Cuddapah on June 22, 23 and 24, 1921. The first president was Sri Akurati Rangannaya Kulu who was a respected caste leader from the community. In the first conference many resolutions were passed in order to improve the social status of the community. An important resolution passed in this conference was to start a *Padmasali Magazine* on behalf of the Sabha.

The second conference was conducted in Mangalgiri on December, 23, 24 and 25, 1923. The important resolutions passed in this session were, to appoint a Committee for the reformation of caste customs and to trace a history of Bhavanarishi. This conference stressed the need for education to reform the caste customs on a secular line. Some of the customs which existed in the community were highly condemned.

The next session was held in Kanchipuram on February 11 and 12, 1924. This conference was presided over by a young leader Shri Tadipatri Sriram Shresthi. Many resolutions were passed for the welfare of local sabhas which stressed the need for caste solidarity at a wider level.

The fourth conference was held at Pedna on April 26 and 27, 1925, under the presidentship of Shri Chenchu Venkat Rangam Shresthi. In this conference, the prime mover of Padmasali Mahasabha, Sri Karyampudi Venkat Krishna Kavi was recognised as the father of the movement and awarded the title of "Padmasali Pitamaha". Resolutions were passed regarding development of handloom industry and stressed the need for starting "Vedic School" to train the Padmasalis to undertake priestly duties for the community members. The fifth conference was arranged at Nellur on April 14 and 15, 1927, under the presidentship of Sri A.K. Chengalrey Shresthi.

The first five conferences were held in the Madras presidency. The next conference was held on September 13, 14 and 15, 1929 in the State of Nizam. The President of this congress was Sri Damodar Krishna Murthy, B.A., B.L., a famous lawyer from Kakinada and the Chairman of Kakinada Municipality. The sabha prepared and submitted a memorandum requesting the then Madras Government to give him a seat in the Madras Assembly. The fifth conference, passed a resolution to start an education fund for the promotion of education among the Padmasalis. Even though the resolution was passed in the fifth conference, no attempts were made to collect any money for the fund till the sixth conference. So the sixth conference, donated an amount of Rs. 116 as an initial contribution to the Secretary of the education fund committee.

Phase III

The first seven conferences were held in the states of Nizam and Madras. Till the seventh Mahasabha, Padmasalis residing in the northern States were not aware of the existence of the Mahasabha. Many prominent leaders from the community visited places like Bombay and Ahmedabad, to explain to the people the importance of the Mahasabha and requested them to take part in the association. During the seventh Mahasabha, few persons from the state of Bombay attended the conference. The eighth Mahasabha was held at Sholapur on May 16, 17, 18 and 19, 1941. Nearly 20,000 people from Ahmednagar, Bombay, Sholapur, Ahmedabad, Hyderabad, Madras and Mysore attended this conference. The president of this conference was Sri Ashanna Iravathi a social worker from Sholapur. Many resolutions were passed during this conference which were aimed at caste reforms and development of handloom industry. For the first time the Mahasabha resolved to prepare a constitution for itself and a committee was appointed for this purpose. Another important resolution was passed by the Mahasabha to request the Government to include the Padmasali community in the backward classes, since the community members were educationally backward.

After the eighth conference, a total of eight Working Committee meetings were held in places like Sholapur, Ahmednagar, Bombay, Sirsilla, Pune and Sindewahi. During the Working Committee meetings resolutions pertaining to social reform and the handloom industry were passed and various personnels from the community were felicitated. In the sixth working committee meeting people from Sindewahi requested to hold the ninth session there, and the working committee accepted their request. After a gap of eight years, the ninth conference was held in Sindewahi on April 21, 22, 1948. This session was chaired by Vaddepathi Vittobagaru.

After the ninth conference, people did not show any interest in holding the next conference. Ashanna Iravathi, from Sholapur, communicated with the leaders of Ahmedabad, Marathwada and Bangalore to hold the next session. A working committee meeting was held at Ahmedabad on December 9, 1961. The leaders from the host city agreed to hold the ninth session. Since the people living in Ahmedabad were mainly mill workers, they found it very difficult to meet the expenses of the conference. So to raise the funds, contributions were collected from Gujarat, Madhya Pradesh,

Karnataka, Maharashtra and Andhra Pradesh. A total amount of Rs. 28,025 was collected from these areas. The tenth session of the sabha was held at Ahmedabad on April 16, 17 and 18, 1971 under the Chairmanship of Ashanna Iravathi. About 10,000 people from Maharashtra, Gujarat, Andhra Pradesh and Karnataka attended the session.

The eleventh session of the sabha was held in Bangalore on December 19 and 20, 1980, in which more than 30,000 people from Tamil Nadu, Kerala, Andhra Pradesh, Maharashtra, Gujarat and Karnataka attended. The President of this association was Sri Venkata Ramanappa, a businessman from Bangalore. This conference has great importance as far as the backward classes movements is concerned. Although steps were taken during the eighth Mahasabha to include the Padmasali caste in the backward classes in the States of Maharashtra and Gujarat, effective measures to press the demand were taken mainly during this conference.

Even though the sabha was started in 1921, within its life span of 62 years, only 11 conferences were held. Within this period, the Mahasabha was neither registered nor had a constitution of its own. The first attempt to prepare a constitution was made during the eighth conference in Sholapur. Accordingly a committee was appointed and in December 1942 a rough draft of the constitution was prepared and passed by the working committee. It was published in the January 1943 issue of the *Padmasali magazines*. However, it was not okayed by the President or the general secretary of the Mahasabha. During the tenth conference, a fresh committee was appointed to prepare a new constitution or revise the existing draft. The constitution was adopted by the Mahasabha, on July 10, 1982. The Mahasabha is not yet registered. According to the latest constitution the aims and objectives are the following:

(a) to make Padmasalis aware of the origin and history of Padmasali community,
(b) to strive for social uplift and development of Padmasalis,
(c) to strive for educational progress of Padmasalis,
(d) to eradicate the evils and outdated customs of Padmasalis,
(e) to strive for cultural development of Padmasalis,
(f) to strive for the improvement and development of Padmasali community's occupation i.e. Handloom industry,
(g) to strive to improve the lot and safeguard the interest of

Padmasalis holding powerlooms,

(h) to encourage and help Padmasalis to take up better avenues of earnings,

(i) to inculcate and develop spiritualism and moral values among the Padmasalis,

(j) to inculcate, promote and strengthen unity among Padmasalis and the sense of individual responsibility towards the community in particular and society in general,

(k) to strive for alround progress and development of the Padmasali community in particular and all other weaker sections of the society in general, and

(l) to promote and strengthen national integrity.

If one compares the constitution of the Nizam Rashtra Padmasali Mahasabha with the constitution which is adopted by All India Padmasali Mahasabha recently, it can be noted that both the constitutions stress the need for social reform in the caste customs and emphasis the development of handloom industry.

Two more national level associations are affiliated to the Central Sabha. They are: (1) All India Padmasali Women's Mahasabha and (2) All India Padmasali Youth Mahasabha. The youth and women's sessions were also held alongwith the Central sabha. The objectives of these two associations are numerous. The educated ladies from the community formed the ladies wing in order to raise the social status of the female folks. The main objectives of the ladies wing are to make the ladies free from traditional restrictions, to educate them to protect them from socio-cultural evils such as early marriage, addiction to drinks, the custom of dowry and to impress upon them the need for family planning. The main object of the youth sabha is to stop the undesirable social practices and traditional customs that persist in the community. Both the associations are striving hard to get the Padmasali community included in the backward classes list of the Central Government so that they will be entitled to government concessions.

Apart from the national level Mahasabhas, there are numerous local sabhas, youth sabhas, and women sabhas, working at the regional level.

The Sabha Organisation

Membership of the Sabha is ascribed and is restricted to the

Padmasalis. In the constitution it is specified that "Padmasali means a person whose hereditary origin is from Bhavanarishi or who accepts Bhrugu Maharshi, Markhandeya Muni or Bhavanarishi as his/her Kuladevatha". From 1921 to 1982, the sabha functioned in an informal way, since it did not have a written constitution of its own. The usual practice was, whenever, the sabha was to be held, a reception committee was formed by selecting members from different parts of the country. The reception committee nominated the office bearers and various committees for conducting the sabha. The tenure of the president of one session was continued till the election of the president for the next session, irrespective of the time gap between the two sessions. Since there was no office for the sabha, all the official documents were kept with the president or secretary of the respective sabhas. The committee meetings were not fixed. Generally the committee meetings were held in the houses of caste elites or in the buildings owned by caste panchayats or local sabhas.

The 1982 constitution provides a set of rules by which the sabha operates. The office bearers are hierarchically graded with a clear cut division of responsibilities and rights. The hierarchical order of office bearers include, one president, four vice-presidents, two general secretaries, a treasurer, and an internal auditor, the working committee consists of a total of 51 members. The president of the Mahasabha is elected by the members of the working committee.

Sabha and Social Reform Activities

The social reform movement among the Padmasalis coincided with the backward classes movement against the ritual and religious monopoly of upper castes which was wide spread in India during the later decades of the 19th century. Sociological and Anthropological literature on reform movement show that the aspiration for the status of the twice born among the lower caste and untouchables, provided the motive for the movement. Padmasalis were never considered untouchables. However, they aspired for the status of twice born castes and claimed superiority over other castes having similar status. The reformation of the customs of the caste began in the later decades of the 19th century. When the first national census was taken various mythological and legendary stories were conveyed to the enumerators in order to demand high social status. In those days, there were several controversies and differences of opinion regarding the practice of caste customs, throughout the state. The Nizam Rashtra Padmasali Mahasabha was formed to put an end to the diverse customs and practices that were prevalent among Padmasalis in various parts of the state. When the sabha was formed its major aim was reformation of caste customs along the lines of the twice born castes. The first Mahasabha which was held in Secunderabad in 1913, introduced wearing of the sacred thread, abstenance from meat, and liquor and banning of re-entry of those who were excommunicated even on payment of fines. According to the decision made by the Sabha many people wore the sacred thread and kept control over dietary habits.

Members of other communities considered the Padmasalis as low in origin due to the practice of certain customs such as meat eating and alcoholism. This activated the caste spirits and many attempts were made to show that they were superior to other castes with similar status. Two examples are given below to support this observation. In the district of Guntur, there is a sacred place called Mangalgiri, where Padmasalis dominated in number. The Laxmi Narayan temple here is very famous. The marriage festival of Laxmi and Narasimha Swamy is celebrated every year on the "Holi" day. The Padmasalis have been offering "Talambru" and "Mangalsutra" for Laxmi and "Madhuparkam" to Hari since time immemorial during this festival. The "Kammas" of the Vasi Reddy clan were the organisers of the marriage festival. They contented that the right to offer "Madhuparkam" should be theirs as they have a higher status than the Padmasalis. The Kammas filed a suit in the court in the year 1918. On behalf of the Padmasalis Sri Karyampudi Venkata Krishanayya appeared before the court and produced some quotations from *Markhandeya Purana*, to show their relations to the Goddess, Laxmi. The stanza depicts the Padmasalis as maternal relatives of Laxmi. Based on the proof forwarded by him, the court passed the verdict in favour of the Padmasalis. As a result, the Padmasalis retained their right to offer the "Madhuparkam" in the temple.

In the same period, another caste Samayakula, claimed that they were superior to Padmasalis. They supported their claim from the content of a book entitled *Markandeya Purana* written by Sri Puranam Kundayya, a member of Samayakula. In this book he has depicted the Padmasalis as people low in origin and the Samayakulam as people of high origin. This controversy lead to rewriting the history of the Padmasali caste. The second conference of the central Mahasabha, appointed a "Kulagrantha Samskarana Committee" to rewrite the history of the Padmasali. The committee was headed by Sri Karyampudi Venkata Krishnayya. He went through the "Puranas" and "Granthas" particularly the *Markhandeya Purana* and prepared a text known as the *Bhavanarishi Mahatmyam*. This text traced the origin of Padmasalis from Bhavanarishi.

The leaders of the Padmasali Mahasabha realised that, they are being considered as low caste due to the existence of caste practices which are taboo to the caste Hindus. So the sabha requested the people of their caste to discard such customs and inculcate good habits so as to raise the prestige of the caste to the level of other high castes. It condemned the practice of child marriage and dowry systems and requested the people to abstain from consuming meat and liquor. They started wearing the sacred thread and Brahmanical rites were adopted, while performing religious and social ceremonies in the community. In order to train the caste members to perform the sacred rituals, in 1925 the Sabha started a "Vedic School" at Battiprolu.

Apart from adopting new caste customs, the sabha made a minor change in the name of the caste. The people of other castes used to mispronounce the caste name in a most humiliating way. They were often addressed as "Julai" (a person without occupation or responsibility) and "sale" (Brother-in-law), which is a swear word. The executive meeting of the sabha decided to change the name into "Padmashali".

Apart from the religious reforms the Padmasali Mahasabha also stressed the secular ones. So the Mahasabha resolved to start an education fund for promoting education among them. The sabha undertook welfare activities for its members. Special emphasis was given to the training of its members in spinning and weaving and the development of handloom industry.

When the All India Padmasali Mahasabha was formed, the Padmasalis residing in various states were debating on the nature of caste reforms. By arranging meetings and by advising people, the Mahasabha exhorted the people to avoid unnecessary debates on these matters, and advised them on the correct ways of reforming the caste rituals. Till the eighth Mahasabha, various measures were taken to implement reforms in matters of caste rituals.

The village of Panchamahal, of the Nizam state, was dominated by Muslims. The Padmasalis residing in this localities had adopted the customs of Muslims, especially in the marriage. Marriage between uncles and nieces was adopted by these Padmasalis. This peculiar customs led to the formation of a separate sub-group within the caste. The Padmasalis residing in this area and practising uncle-niece marriage are known as Panchamahal Padmasalis. Due to this disparity in the caste customs, marriage between Padmasalis and Panchamahal Padmasalis is prohibited. The Nizam Rashtra Padmasali Mahasabha condemned this custom and tried various measures to eradicate the cultural practices among the community members. However, it was the All India Padmasali Mahasabha who took firm steps to eradicate this custom. At the eighth All India Padmasali Mahasabha, a sub-committee was appointed to study the difference in the caste customs. After the survey, the committee reported that, the Panchamahal area was dominated by Muslims and therefore they adopted the Muslim customs of marriage. The Mahasabha exhorted the people to give up such customs, so that the homogeneity of the community would strengthen group solidarity and unity. Due to the efforts of the Mahasabha, the practice was discontinued. Today the Padmasalis and Panchamahal Padmasalis inter marry.

Till 1950s the Padmasali Panchayats operating in different parts of the country ostracised and penalised its members for performing widow marriage. The youth wing of the Mahasabha, worked effectively to promote widow marriages among the community members. The youth leaders assured full cooperation and safeguarded to those who suffered at the hands of the chiefs of caste panchayats for arranging widow marriage. The All India Padmasali Mahasabha took up several cases of harassment of people for practising widow remarriages. The sabha appointed a committee in the year 1946 to help those who have been excommunicated on account of widow marriage. The Mahasabha passed several resolutions to initiate widow marriage and assured its full support to those who practised it.

Padmasalis who came to Hyderabad from villages had to stay in lodges and other places for want of a proper place to live. So the Nizam Rashtra Padmasali Mahasabha constructed a building which is used as a Padmasali hostel and library. A well wisher from the community contributed a sizable amount for the construction of the building. The Central sabha does not have any immovable property of its own. Usually the local associations provide school, college and hostel facilities for its members.

The sabha also worked for the development of handloom industry, the traditional occupation of the community and took measures to train the members in the art of weaving handlooms. The Sabha pressurised the government and the textile departments to supply adequate amount of cotton and thread to the weavers.

Till 1950s the central sabha was very active in reforming the caste customs in the sacred and secular lines. Now-a-days reform activities aimed at Sanskritisation has been stopped. Although local sabhas occasionally pursue this goal. Today, the major activity of the central sabha is social welfare. The sabha has taken steps to discourage child marriages, alcoholism, and wrong notion about family planning and dowry.

Sabha and Backwardness

The eighth conference helped to unite all the Padmasali migrants residing in the northern and southern states, and to strengthen the horizontal solidarity among the caste members residing in different parts of the country. At this conference the sabha for the first time, requested the Government to include the Padmasalis all over India among the backward classes so that they can avail of the concessions given to the backward classes. The collective mobilization, to get the community registered in the backward classes list, gained momentum with the advent of Independence. When the committee to frame the constitution of India was formed, the sabha made many attempts to get a member from this community included in the constitutional Assembly. The working committee sent several telegrams to national leaders with requests to include the Padmasali community members in the assembly. But these attempts did not succeed.

The ninth and tenth conferences, focussed attention primarily on backward class movements. The first Backward Classes Commission report in 1950, categorised Padmasalis throughout India among backward classes. However, the Central Government did not accept the recommendations of the commission on the ground that no criteria had been applied to identify the backward classes. When the Central Government gave power to the state governments to determine the backward classes in their respective states most of the state governments appointed their own committee. In all the Southern states, viz. Andhra Pradesh, Karnataka, Kerala and Tamil Nadu, Padmasalis are placed among the other backward classes by the respective state governments. The percentage of government job reserved for all the backward classes in these states is high: Andhra Pradesh 25 per cent, Karnataka 40 per cent, Kerala 25 per cent and Tamil Nadu 50 per cent, whereas some of the northern states have reserved lesser percentage example Maharashtra 14 per cent, Uttar Pradesh 15 per cent, Jammu & Kashmir 42 per cent and Bihar 26 per cent (Singh, 1982 : 160). The immigrant Padmasalis residing in the states of Gujarat and Maharashtra, are considered as Other Backward Community (OBC). The percentage of reservation enjoyed by the OBC's in these two states is also very low. In Maharashtra only 10 per cent of the jobs are reserved for other backward classes, which includes 188 communities. The disparity in the percentage of reservations enjoyed by the Padmasalis residing in the southern and northern states, strengthened the backward class movements.

In the 1970s many local sabhas sprung up in these two states with the intention of getting the community included among the backward classes. Some of these associations worked independently of the Mahasabha, to work in order to achieve their objective. They even demanded the Government to include their community among Scheduled Castes or Scheduled Tribes. They sought help from political leaders from the community as well as from outside. The main contention of Padmasalis residing in these two states was that they are not permanently settled in one locality and that they move from one place to another frequently. The Padmasalis, residing in these two states, demanded the respective state governments to list them with the nomadic or denotified tribes.

Since the community was aspiring for a high social status in the Hindu social structure, there were diverse opinions among the Mahasabha leaders regarding the demands. The eleventh Mahasabha took up this issue. The old caste elites did not agree with the suggestion of including Padmasalis among the scheduled castes and tribes. However, due to the pressure of the younger persons, and considering the backwardness of the community members residing these two states, the Mahasabha agreed to make efforts to place the Padmasalis among the scheduled tribes rather than scheduled castes. The central sabha requested all the Padmasalis residing in the country to extend their full support and cooperation in getting the Padmasali community in these two states included among the scheduled tribes.

Within the span of past five to ten years, several youth Mahasabhas have emerged in Maharashtra and Gujarat. The main aim of these sabhas is to place their community among the scheduled tribes throughout India in general and in Maharashtra and Gujarat in particular. In Maharashtra, three local sabhas have taken firm steps to pressurise the government. They are (1) Maharashtra Padmasali Samaj Ekta Sangh — Bombay, (2) Akil Padmasali Samaj Sangharsha Samiti, Bombay and (3) Padmasali Magas Varga Kruti Samiti, Sholapur with branches all over in Maharashtra.

The Maharashtra Padmasali Samaj Ekta Sangh issued circulars to their caste brethren, negating the mythological stories of Padmasali origin, and pointing out that they belong to the aboriginal tribes because they are numerically small, economically poor, socially and culturally deprived, politically powerless and illiterate. The circular argued that the community fulfilled the criteria adopted by the government of India under Sections 15(4), 16(4) and 343 of the constitution for consideration as a scheduled tribe. It also demanded that the Mandal Commission's report should not be accepted by the Government unless the Padmasalis and similar castes are declared scheduled tribes by the Government.

The Padmasali Samaj Sangharsha Samiti held a public meeting at Worli on June 27, 1981, and demanded the inclusion of the community in the list of Denotified or Nomadic Tribes in Maharashtra. They pursued this matter by holding meetings and mobilising Padmasalis at various places and states. The Samiti submitted a memorandum to the Central and State governments and took a delegation to Shri G.P. Kuchan M.P., requested him to bring pressure on the Central Government to get their demands passed in Parliament.

The Padmasali Central Sabha does not aim at the political mobilization of the community. However, political mobilization of the community is achieved by the local sabhas. In Maharashtra, the local associations lead by Mr. G.P. Kuchan, M.P. have managed to politically mobilise the community. A separate Backward Classes Action Committee was formed with 53 members at Sholapur, Maharashtra in 1978, under his presidentship with branches in different parts of Maharashtra. The main objective of this committee is to work exclusively for the inclusion of the Padmasali community in the scheduled tribes list. The demands of this committee include the relaxation of the upper age limit in Government jobs, job reservations concession in education and reservation of seats in educational institutions. In March, 1978, members of Magas Varga Kruti Samiti and the Maharashtra Rajaya Padmasali Yuvak Sanghatana and many other community members kept away from their work and organised political rallies throughout Maharashtra. They submitted memorandums to the district Collectors, the Maharashtra Government and the Central Government demanding inclusions of their community in the Scheduled Caste list.

In February 1980, under the auspices of the Backward Class Action Committee representatives from Sholapur, Ahmednagar and Pune met the Backward Classes Commission (Mandals) and submitted a memorandum explaining the reasons for inclusions of the community in the list of backward classes. Nearly 1,000 people from the above mentioned places also marched through the city of Pune and submitted a memorandum to the District Collector.

In the same year Mr. G.P. Kuchan, M.P. formed the Sholapur Padmasali Yuvak Sanghatana, became the president of Maharashtra Rajya Padmasali Yuvak Sanghatana and led a representation of 62 members from different parts of Maharashtra, and met the then Chief Minister, Sri A.R. Anthulay to demand reservation facilities for the community.

On October 5, 1980, the first conference of Marathwada Padmasali Mahasabha was held at Nanded. During this conference nearly 1,000 members of this association met the Collector of Nanded district and demanded inclusion of their community in the backward class list.

The Padmasalis of Maharashtra joined hands with other OBC caste aspiring for Backward Class status, like Mali, Kunbi, Bhandari, Koli, Dhangar, Shimpi, Vanjari and Sonars. All these communities are working jointly in order to press their demand. The Padmasalis from Maharashtra sent their representative to participate in the national conference of the Backward Classes which was held in Delhi in December, 1981 and in Madras 1982.

Like the Padmasalis residing in Maharashtra, the Padmasalis in Gujarat, also active in demanding Backward Class status. On October 18, 1981, the "Gujarat Padmasali Jynata Samastha", convened a meeting of Padmasalis from various parts of Gujarat, including Surat, Ahmednagar and Navasari. The meeting was presided over by Sri Sidram Kota. The details of the Mandal Commission's report were explained to the community members and a memorandum was prepared and presented to the President and the Prime Minister. In this meeting, they formed the "Gujarat Padmasali Samaj Sangharsha Samiti" to work exclusively for this purpose in the state. The office bearers of this association met Janata Party leaders and the former external affairs minister, Shri A.B. Vajpayee, to seek their help to get the community included in the category of scheduled tribes. Similarly on November 28, 1981 the office bearers of the Samiti met Sri

Maganbai Barot, the then Deputy Finance Minister of India, and discussed the communities demand with him. Unlike in Maharashtra in Gujarat there are no political leaders from the community and therefore they pursue this matter with the help of local and national political leaders belonging to the ruling party as well as opposition parties.

By 1980 the central sabha also started taking interest in the movement. When the second Backward Classes Commission was appointed, the Mahasabha sent a delegation, consisting of the president, vice president, general secretary, and other committee members to Delhi. Shri G.S. Kuchan, M.P. was requested to lead the delegation to Delhi. The delegation met with the Prime Minister and other concerned ministers and discussed their demands. On March 30, 1983, the Central Home Minister, called a meeting of all the Chief Ministers to consider the report of the Mandal Committee. The President of the Mahasabha directed all the regional sabhas to present their opinion regarding the Mandal Commission Report at the meeting of the Chief Ministers.

The reference group of Padmasalis have shifted from the twice born castes to the Backward Classes with the advent of Indian Independence. The disparity in the percentage of reservation enjoyed by the Padmasalis in the southern and northern states, triggered off the movement in Maharashtra and Gujarat. The regional associations of Padmasalis in Gujarat and Maharashtra strongly demanded Backward Class status to the community. In order to strengthen their demands they are now demanding inclusion of their community among the Scheduled Castes or Tribes. Sabha being primarily constituted by Padmasalis from the South did not initially take up the demands of the Padmasalis of Maharashtra and Gujarat. The Padmasali Mahasabha and the local sabhas are not politically oriented. However, they have now a political role to play. The Padmasalis from Maharashtra have joined hands with similar castes who are aspiring for the status of Backward Classes. The struggle for the status of Backward Classes is continuing at present.

Sabha and Periodicals

Caste periodical is one of the important media which helps to reinforce contact among the central Mahasabha, the local sabhas, and the widely dispersed caste members. It carries news and conveys the aspirations, achievement and the latest development in the community at a wider level. This also helps as a means to motivate and inspire the caste members in their struggle for political recognition as a Backward caste.

The first ethnic periodical, the *Padmasali Magazine*, was published from Apayya Raupeta (Nizam State) under the editorship of Nukula Chinayya in December, 1921. It was published in Telugu and therefore Padmasalis residing in Nizam and Madras states benefited from it. It was not very popular among the Padmasalis residing in other states. When the Mahasabha organised its first meeting in the state of Bombay in 1941, many people from this state came to know of the existence of this ethnic periodical and became interested in it. Following the conference, a Marathi section was incorporated into the magazine for the benefit of the Padmasalis residing in the State of Bombay. However, by 1950 the publication of this journal was stopped because of financial loss. During its life a span of ten years its circulation did not go beyond 400 copies.

In the late 70's and early 80's many caste elites from different parts of the country came forward to start new periodicals. Today there are four popular journals three of which are published from south India and one from Maharashtra. The details of these journals are given in the Table 5.2.

TABLE 5.2: Details of Caste Journals

Place of Publication	Title of the Journal	Language	Year of starting of Publication	Frequency
Madras	Padmajyoti	Telugu	1978	Monthly
Bangalore	Padmasali	Kannada	1979	Trimonthly
Nanded (Maharashtra)	Pakshik Padmasali	Telugu & Marathi	1980	Fortnightly
Hyderabad	Padmajyoti	Telugu	1977	Monthly

Pakshik Padmasali and Padmajyoti are published in two languages: Telugu and Marathi. The other two journals are published in Telugu and Kannada.

No attempt has been made to analyse the contents of these journals in detail. However it is noted that a major portion of these journals is dedicated to news of the community. The journal *Padmasali* which was originally published from Nizam state and later on from Sholapur, contains article mainly on the proceedings of the Mahasabha and local sabhas. Articles written by caste elites propagate reforms in the caste customs. Various articles deal with the handloom industry, which is their traditional occupation. The major part of the journals covers the following heads: proceedings of the Mahasabha and the local sabhas, caste reform activities, socio-economic and political development of the community, their aspiration interest and problems, like histories of certain caste elites, literary articles, short stories, caste based articles, addresses of caste elites, problems faced by the handloom industry, details of cooperative handloom societies, special notices and announcements and matrimonial columns.

Sabha and Development of Handloom Industry

The Padmasalis are traditionally handloom workers. Right from the inception of the Mahasabha one of its main aim has been to development of the handloom industry. In the constitutions of the Nizam Rashtra Padmasali and All India Padmasali Mahasabha give special importance to the development of handloom industry. From 1880 onwards, due to industrialization and import of foreign cloth, handloom industry has suffered a severe setback. During the early decades of the 20th century handloom weavers faced a lot of problems especially in the supply of cotton and yarn. The government and textile department did not take adequate measures to supply these to the weavers. The Nizam Rashtra Mahasabha requested the government and textile department to supply adequate quantity of cotton and yarn to the workers. However, the Sabha asked the people to start co-operative societies and become members of the society in order to overcome the problems.

The history of handloom industry in India had not yet been published and therefore, the All India Padmasali Mahasabha appointed a committee of five members including Sri Karyampudi Nagendra Rao, B.A.B.T. and Sri Tadiparthi Srikandam to write the same. The Committee wrote a book on handloom industry entitled *Indian Cloth Industry*. This book records the past and present history of the handloom industry. Several problems of the industry have been discussed suggested remedial measures.

In 1940, The British Government had appointed a committee in order to undertake a survey of industrial and economic development in each state under the presidentship of Purushottam Das Thakur Das. The Mahasabha took care that all the handloom societies submitted their report to the committee. In 1941, the Government appointed a "fact finding committee" under the presidentship of P.J. Thomas, in order to find out the problems of the handloom industry. The Mahasabha requested all the handloom industries to fill properly the questionnaire distributed by the committee. The Mahasabha appointed a committee to study the problem of handloom industry in India, and submitted a 60 page report in English to the "fact finding committee".

In almost all the Mahasabhas, resolutions were passed requesting the government to protect the handloom industry from mills, since the handloom product was not able to compete with the mill product. In the eighth Mahasabha it was resolved that persons wearing mill cloths should not be allowed to become members of the executive committee. During the proceedings of the Mahasabha it is customary to open an exhibition of handloom cloths wherever the conference was held.

The local sabhas also demanded the government to take various measures to protect the handloom industry from other cloth industries and to supply proper cotton and financial assistance to handloom industries. The western Maharashtra Padmasali Mahasabha, Ahmednagar, on 7th March, 1979 demanded financial assistance to handloom workers and requested the government to reserve 90 per cent of seats in spinning technical institutes to the weaving castes.

Today the task of the Mahasabha has become easier, since there are many national level, state level and regional level co-operative societies and associations, which take care of the handloom and powerloom industry in the country. In each state there are numerous co-operative societies which work for the development and improvement of the handloom industry. Moreover, today many of the community members have left their traditional occupation and are searching new avenues for their livelihood. Even the central sabha is encouraging the members to take up other means of livelihood as the handloom industry is not prospering.

Summary

The organized communal activities of Padmasalis in Hyderabad started in the wake of 20th century, initially with the formation of local associations meant mainly for celebrating religious functions. Subsequently by 1913, statewide associations developed which mainly worked for Sankritising the caste customs. These associations had several attempts to eliminate the outdated customs of the caste and worked to raise the community's status. Attempts were also made to bring about reforms in dietary habits and the people were requested to wear sacred thread. Along the reform activities the Sabha also worked for the welfare of its members.

By 1921, this association developed into a national level association with the aim of reforming the caste customs both on sacred and secular lines. The sabha also tried to claim superiority for its caste over other castes having similar caste status. This was attempted in terms of establishing their mythical origin and relation to gods. Many attempts were made to reform the caste customs on secular lines. The differences in practice of caste customs had led to the formation of sub-groups within the community. The sabha tried to eliminate differences in caste practices among sub-groups. To a certain extent this helped to make the community homogeneous. The sabha advised the Panchayat Chiefs to promote reform activities on secular lines. It also safeguarded the interest of its members who were penalised by panchayat on account of reform activities.

Till 1940, their reference group for mobility was the twice born caste. But after Independence, their reference group became backward classes, in order to avail of the reservation facilities offered to them. The backward classes movement gained momentum in Maharashtra and Gujarat when the quantum of reservation enjoyed by the Padmasalis residing in the southern states was higher than their counter parts in northern India. Numerous local sabhas sprung up especially in the States of Maharashtra and Gujarat to demand the inclusion of the community in the backward classes list. Some of them negated the existing mythological stories of the origin of the Padmasalis and tried to establish that they are aboriginal tribes. They pressurised the central sabha to work for placing them among the scheduled castes/tribes category. As the central sabha was aspiring for the status of twice born castes for Padmasalis, there was disagreement among the leaders of the central and local sabhas regarding the identification of the community with scheduled castes. On account of the pressure from the younger generation the central sabha started to work for placing the community among scheduled tribes rather than scheduled castes.

The caste elites who led the central sabha were mainly traditional leaders with moderate education, except a lawyer who took keen interest in promoting education by starting an education fund. The caste elites were neither politically influential nor was the sabha politically motivated, during the pre-Independence period. Political elites have not taken any interest in the central sabha affairs. But during the 1970s and after the local and the central sabha have been seeking the help of political leaders from the community and outside to get their community included in the backward class category. In Maharashtra a member of the Parliament from the community has been mobilising the youths and exerting political pressure to fulfil their objective.

A comparison of the aims and objectives of the sabha of Kanya Kubja Brahmin (Khare, 1970 : 47) the Nadars, (Hardgrave, 1969 : 132) the Kurmis (Verma, 1979 : 48-49) and that of Padmasalis shows that they have several similarities. However, the associations of these communities have evolved under different historical circumstances and with different initial motives. Except the Kanya Kubja sabha, initial activities of the other sabhas were directed to reforming the caste customs on the line of twice born castes. Later on their reference group changed to that of the backward classes so as to gain constitutional benefits. All these sabhas stressed reform activities on the secular line. Kurmie and Padmasali Mahasabha stressed the development of their traditional occupations. The Nadar Sangam did not give any importance for the development of their traditional occupation viz. Toddy tapping, however, it stressed the promotion of commercial enterprises among the community members. The Kanya Kubja Sabha's aims were directed to solving institutional problems rather than caste mobility.

Within the span of 62 years, the sabha held only eleven sessions. There was no regularity in holding the conference and it was held at irregular intervals. General body meetings are seldom held. Meetings are generally held in houses or temples owned by the caste panchayats or local sabhas. There is no property or bank account for the sabha. Since there is no permanent office all the official documents are kept with the president or secretary of the successive sabha. Although the sabha adopted a constitution in 1982, formal registration is yet to be done. In short, the sabha is less formal in its structure and mainly functions on the basis of traditional norms and consensus.

6

CONCLUSIONS

In the preceding chapters, I have tried to analyse the role of ethnic associations in the process of urbanization. Several ethnic associations have been studied from a historical perspective, taking into account the process of Indian Urbanization, during the pre-colonial, colonial and post-colonial periods. In doing so, I have attempted to evaluate the existing theories on voluntary associations and assess their applicability to the Indian Urban Context. In the western and African contexts, it was contended, that due to urbanization, the traditional forms of associations are unable to perform the intended functions and therefore, voluntary associations proliferate in order to compensate the functions rendered by traditional forms of associations.

The point of departure for the present analysis of ethnic associations is the classical assumptions that primary groups are generally replaced by secondary groups in the urban context. Implicit in the above assumption is an evolutionary approach which has dominated the scientific literature on voluntary associations. This has led to a dichotomisation of voluntary associations belonging to the traditional and the modern. The analysis presented in this thesis suggests that such dichotomisation is an over simplification of complex urban phenomenon. This over simplification, has resulted in terminological confusion in social sciences on associations in the urban context. Even though, several associations in the urban social system tend to show some characteristics, of the voluntary association, it would be inappropriate to characterise all urban associations particularly those based on ethnicity as voluntary associations. All the 71 associations of a regional immigrant community, which have been subjected to the present enquiry are organizations based on ethnicity such as village of origin, sub caste, caste, religion and language. While all the associations perform certain primary group functions, none of them is a purely modern voluntary organization.

Some of the ethnic associations do incorporate certain features of modern voluntary associations. To start with we have analysed 20 caste panchayats in order to find out the changes undergone by them over time. The typology which emerged out of the analysis of caste panchayats at three levels viz. organization, activity and democratization shows that fused panchayats have structural functional characteristics similar to those of the village caste panchayats. However, they are not the exact replica of village caste panchayats. The second type, the transitional panchayat is in a stage of transition from tradition to modern. Both traditional and modern organizational features do co-exist in this type. Differentiated panchayats exhibit several features of modern organizations and they have lost some of the traditional features. Even though, certain modern organizational features are incorporated in this type of panchayats in actual practice they are not strictly followed. Only those practices which are necessary for the smooth functioning of caste panchayats in the changing context are followed.

There are several factors responsible for initiating changes in the structure and function of these associations. The process of urbanization and the conditions of life in a city, indeed, contribute to this change. In addition several organizational features of ethnic associations tend to adjust and adapt to the restrictions imposed by the wider administrative structure, and legal machinery at the level of the city, state and nation. For instance, a marriage sanctioned by the caste panchayat in the traditional style is not strictly legal, unless, it is registered at the marriage registrar's office. Similarly the caste panchayats cannot solve all the disputes within the community on its own accord and keep away the legal machinery. Another example is that of the registration of ethnic associations. The ethnic associations have to be registered, if the objectives pursued by them come under the objectives listed in the societies Registration Act and/or the Public Trust Act. A registered association should have a written constitution and a democratic set up of official body. The changes in the structure of caste panchayat on account of registration is evident if we compare the three types of caste panchayats. While the fused type of panchayats are not registered under the Public Trust Act, nearly eighty per cent of the transitional panchayats are registered and all the differentiated panchayats are registered. The fused panchayats retain all the structural and functional characteristics of the village panchayats. The transitional panchayats show both traditional and modern authority structure, and a mixture of traditional and modern organizational features. The differentiated panchayats show democratized authority and mostly modern organizational structure.

The changes in the organizational structure and functions of associations are affected by the wider socio-political environment. The changing power structure of the democratic Indian polity finds its way into the structure of ethnic associations. On account of this, it may appear as if the associations are progressing from traditional to modern. In fact, these associations are operating on the basis of ethnic ties and traditional communal unity and are attempting to adjust and adapt to the socio-political environment. The capacity of ethnic associations to adjust and adapt to changing social environment is clear from the data on multi caste panchayat.

A multi caste panchayat was formed in the later decades of the 19th century by uniting 12 lower caste Telugu immigrant communities. This was necessitated by the fact that the number of migrant belonging to each caste group was very small, during this period. But by the early decades of the 20th century, the number of immigrants increased and the multicaste panchayats split into several caste associations. The point which I wish to emphasise is that the form and content of ethnic associations undergo changes depending on the changing social environment. This adjustment could as well be towards the direction of modernization, in so far as the socio-political environment demands it. In other contexts the changes may take other directions.

The adaptive potentiality of ethnic associations is very explicit in the data described in chapter four. The classification of ethnic associations presented in this chapter, viz. active, passive, transformed and disbanded is based essentially on the nature of adaptations they have been able to make, in order to cope with the changing situations over time. While their major function is to promote adjustment and adaptation of the immigrants in the city, they change in form and content to accommodate the complex urban way of life. A few of the active associations were formed during the early stages of migration and settlement, while some others were formed after the industrialization of Pune. They promote educational and co-operative activities, provide recreational and religious facilities and look after the welfare of the community members.

In addition and most importantly, they are resilient enough to accommodate competing ethnic groups within their fold and thus perform integrative functions. All the associations identified as active have been able to adjust and adapt to the changing situations and meet the fast changing demands of the immigrants life in the city. Some of the active associations become passive, once their intended functions have been fulfilled. All the passive associations were active when the influx of immigrants was heavy. The passive associations either transform themselves by undergoing structural and functional changes or die off and disappear from the scene. The transformed associations are very resilient and they change form and content in order to adopt and adjust to the changing situations. All the associations except one, which have categorised and disbanded, were formed before the industrialization of Pune. The one which survived performs expressive functions, while others were instrumental in nature. These associations, disappeared from the scene due to various factors like fission, fusion, socio-political change, deculturation, and attainment of intended functions.

The type and function of associations change with the process of urbanization. However, ethnic associations in India are not transforming from primary to secondary associations to the extent that the western and African models would have made us to believe. The western and African models suggest that in the initial stages of migration, ethnic associations act as adaptive mechanisms and in later stages they become purely recreational and as immigrants become increasingly urbanized the importance of primary associations would diminishes. The historical data on several associations and their classification present in this study do not show that all of them end up as purely recreational associations. They are, in fact, continuously changing their form and content in order to cope with the changing conditions. Moreover, many active associations perform several primary functions despite urbanization and improvement in standard of living. Our finding is that ethnic associations formed during the initial stages of migration help the immigrants to adjust and adapt to a new cultural setting, and with the passage of time they themselves undergo adaptive changes to cope with changing situations. In this process, some associations several integrative and welfare functions in addition to recreational.

Various terminologies have been used by scholars to refer ethnically based immigrants associations in the city. Such associations have been referred to as: Common interest associations (Norbeck, 1977), Ethnic Associations (Lloyd, 1967), Ethnic Unions (Smock,

1971), Improvement Associations (Ottenbergh, 1955), Improvement Unions (Uchendu, 1965) and Traditionalist Association (Lloyd, 1967).

In the Indian Urban Context these associations have been treated under the general category of voluntary associations (Singh, 1975; Lewandowski, 1980). Some scholars have pointed out that the ethnic associations fall under an intermediate category between traditional and modern (Khare, 1970; Verma, 1979). Various scholars have adopted different operational definitions taking one or the other characteristics of these associations. The lack of an all agreeable definition have led to considerable terminological ambiguity and confusion regarding these associations. This is on account of the fact that the ethnically based immigrants' associations are undergoing structural and functional modifications in the changing urban situations. Some of these have incorporated some characteristics of voluntary associations, while others maintain their traditional features. The findings of the present study suggests that the change from traditional to modern is an adaptation to the changing needs and often to satisfy the rules laid down by the Government. Even associations which have incorporated some of the modern organizational features show several primary group characteristics. Comparative data on the characteristics of primary group, secondary associations and modern organizations extracted from sociological literature, and various kinds of associations analysed in this study substantiate this claim. The data are presented in Table 6.1.

The basic features of primary associations are strong among all ethnic associations except the regional associations and the caste sabha. In the case of the regional association, and the caste sabha, the primary group features are weak and secondary group features are strong. The regional association is organized on the basis of linguistic unity, which in the Indian context provides a wider level of ethnic identity, as compared to association based on stronger identity principles such as kinship, village of origin, sub-caste and caste. Nair (1983) provides a model of ethnic identity in the Indian Urban Context. The model suggests that the rigidity of group definition and ethnic identity are strongest at the caste level. They become increasingly weaker at the level of religion, language, social class and nationality. Because of this, rigidity and clarity of group definition of regional association is not as strong as in the case of other association. The regional association is formed by people belonging to different caste, sub-castes and class, but speaking the same language.

TABLE 6.1: Comparative Data on characteristics of primary, secondary and modern organisation and ethnic associations

Sl. No. Primary Association	Secondary Association	Modern Organisation	Ethnic Associations			
			Differentiated Panchayat*	Active Association	Regional Association	Caste Sabha
1	2	3	4	5	6	7
1. Strong in Group Feeling	Loosely affiliated	Loosely affiliated	Strong in group feeling	Strong in group feeling	Moderate in group feeling	Moderate in group feeling
2. Based on primary ties	Secondary ties	Technical norms and rules	Primary ties	Primary ties	Primary ties operating on the basis of language identity	Primary ties, operating on the basis of caste identity
3. Face to face relations	Impersonal	Impersonal	Face to face relation	Face to face relauon	Face to face relations to some extent	Face to face relations to some extent
4. Less specialised in functions	Specialised in functions	Highly specialised in functions	Less specialised in functions	Specialised in function	Not specialised in function	Specialised in function
5. Communal in function	Semi Communal/ Professional	Highly Professional	Communal in function	Communal in function	Communal in function	Communal in function
6. Membership Ascriptive (inclusive)	Achieved (exclusive)	Achieved (Restricted)	Ascriptive (inclusive)	Ascriptive	Ascriptive	Ascriptive (based on caste cluster)

(Contd.)

TABLE 6.1 *(Contd.)*

1	2	3	4	5	6	7
7. Authority Traditional	Democratic	Bureaucratic	Democratic	Democratic operating on the basis of consensus	Democratic Follows ballot voting etc.	Democratic operating on the basis of consensus
8. No written rules and regulations	Present	Present	Have written rules and regulations, but not strictly followed	In some cases written rules & regulations present, but not strictly followed	Present. Follows them strictly	Have written rules & regulations. Follows to a certain extent Informal norms dominates
9. No systematic division of labour	Systematic division of labour present	Present	Present	In some cases no systematic division of labour informal roles dominates	Present	Present
10. Traditional hierarchy	Hierarchical	Hierarchical	Hierarchical	Clear & in certain cases incipient	Clear	Clear
11. Officials are not paid	Officials are not paid	Officials are paid	Officials are not paid	Officials are not paid	Not paid	Not paid
12. Mainly oral Communication	Written Communication	Written Communication	Oral Communication	Written Communication	Written Communication	Written Communication

Note: Characteristics of Fused Transitional Panchayats are not included in this table. They show more stronger primary group relations. Only characteristics of the changing caste panchayats viz. the Differentiated Panchayat is presented in the table.

Similarly, the caste sabha also shows many secondary characteristics. Although, the membership in caste sabha is based on an ascriptive criteria viz. caste, the sabha operates at the national level which ultimately weakens the caste identity. Caste as a significant in group has a regional connotation. In other words, the common cultural identity that castes share become significant only within a sub cultural context. Caste identity at a regional level or at a national level do not provide strong and clear group definition. People belonging to the same caste but from different cultural region are not likely to have strong ethnic identity unlike a caste group from the same cultural region.

Membership in all these associations is based on certain ascriptive criteria. Although, membership in some active associations is open for other community members on a voluntary basis, this number of members from other communities in these associations is very negligible. Sometimes the facilities provided by some of these associations are also extended to other community members. This is only a temporary mechanism to maintain friendly relations and peaceful co-existence of ethnic groups within the city. The negligible percentage of members from other ethnic groups in these associations does not undermine the ethnic character or the primary group features of these associations. In so far as the membership in these associations is based on ascriptive criteria such as caste, region-of-origin, religion and language, and their functions are directed towards certain ethnic groups, they are not in the strict sense voluntary associations.

A well defined democratic official body is strictly operational only in the case of regional association. Some of the active associations and differentiated panchayats have incorporated some of the modern organizational features, such as registration, and democratic official set up. However, in actual practice ethnic associations do not follow them strictly. Only in the case of the regional association follows ballot voting and democratization. In other types of ethnic associations democratization exist only superficially. They operate mostly on the basis of consensus.

The degree of informality of an association depends upon the level of its operation. An associations operating on the basis of kinship, village-of-origin, sub-caste, and caste shows many primary group features and follow traditional pattern of behaviour. Whereas associations formed on the basis of language tend to share more secondary characteristics.

The formation, nature, preservation and change in ethnic association can be accounted for by the peculiar features of Indian Urbanization. Indian Urbanization is characterized by distinct stages and not parallel to western and African process of urbanization. Indian Urbanization shows three distinct stages: Pre-colonial, colonial and post-colonial. Each stage of urbanization corresponds to a particular pattern of migration and settlement and the nature of associations formed at each stage differs.

During the pre-colonial period, migration and settlement was temporary and the chances of formation of ethnic associations were minimal. The stream of migration increased considerably during the colonial period. Urbanization during the initial stages of the colonial rule was marked by the influx of large number of lower caste members. They migrated to cities to pursue their traditional occupations. The pattern of migration may be characterised as mass migration and chain migration, and the settlement as chain settlement and gravitation group settlement. The associations formed as a result of chain migration and settlement was based on kinship, village and sub caste identity. Later on they fused together and formed associations at caste level. The reverse is this pattern with regard to ethnic associations formed as a result of gravitation group settlement. Here ethnic associations were formed at the multi-caste level. These associations split up at individual caste level.

The migration during the post-colonial period is marked by the influx of middle and upper castes and middle class people. Individual migration is the pattern in Indian cities which are rapidly industrializing. In addition to individual migration, chain migration and settlement and gravitation group settlement also continue to some extent. Individual migration and shortage of accommodation in the ethnic enclave are responsible for scattering of ethnic groups within the city. As a result of scattered settlement, ethnic associations which are formed during this period operate on the basis of wider identity principle, such as caste, religion, social class and language. Such associations are dominated and managed by middle and upper class people.

Our conclusion in this study is that the changes or modifications that are observed in ethnic associations over time are adaptive responses to the modern conditions of pluralist democracy which is rapidly urbanizing and industrializing. The use of the concept of adaptation to explain change may lead to certain legitimate conceptual problems. Is the concept of adaptation adequate enough to take stock of change? The concept of adaptation tend to emphasise structural stability rather than change. However, the use of the concept in this study does not consider adaptation as a static phenomena. Instead adapting response of ethnic associations to the fast changing conditions in the city is viewed as a continuous process. This process has been demonstrated by historical data on ethnic associations presented in this study.

To those scholars who are committed to an evolutionary model (tradition to modern) the use of the concept of adaptive response to take stock of change in ethnic associations may appear even more inappropriate. It may be pointed out that the concept of assimilation which envisages the breakdown of traditional culture of ethnic groups and their meager into a dominant group has been the product of such as evolutionary framework. Empirical evidence from all over the world has questioned the validity of assimilation model. The fact is that ethnic groups do maintain their separate identity despite contrary expectations. There is no denying the fact that ethnic associations tend to loose some of its primary characteristics and adapt some of the secondary features in the Indian Urban Context. Yet, it would be inappropriate to think of this purely as a progression from tradition to modern. Overwhelming evidence is available in the Indian context to demonstrate the primary nature of ethnic identity in the urban context. The changes that various ethnic associations have undergone that have been documented is the study should, in my view, be regarded as adaptive response to the modern conditions of a pluralist democracy and industrial urbanization that the country has opted for.

APPENDIX

INTERVIEW GUIDE

1. Name and address of the association.
2. When did it start? (Year, month, with date).
3. By whom? (Name and position now and then).
4. Where it was started?
5. For what reason (What are the aims and objectives of the association).
6. Is it registered? Yes/No.
7. Is there any office for the association? Yes/No. If Yes, office is owned by the association or rented. Owned/Rented/Free/Any other.

Members

1. How many members are on the roll?
2. What are the criteria for membership?
3. What are the types of membership?
4. What is the membership fees?
5. Is there any monthly or yearly subscription? If yes how much?
6. How many of the members do you say are active?
7. What do you mean by "active members"?
8. How does one become a member? By invitation, then application etc.
9. Is there a waiting period for the aspiring members?
10. Do you require the approval by the central committee before they are admitted as a full-fledged member?
11. Have you ever refused membership to anybody in your association? Yes/No. If yes on what ground?
12. Did anybody voluntarily leave the association? Yes/No. If yes what was the reason?
13. Did you expel anybody from your association membership. Yes/No. If yes specify the reason?

14. To which class (Upper, Middle, Lower) majority of the members belong to?
15. Do many of the members of your association belong to other association also?
16. From which area in the city majority of the members are drawn. Specify the area.
17. Do you know each and every member of the association personally?

Office Bearers

1. How many office bearers are there?
2. What are the office bearers do you have?
3. What are the designation and educational qualifications of the office bearers?
4. Find the office bearers' position in the society?
5. What is the method of selection of office bearers? By inheritance, By nomination, By election.
6. When is the election held? What is the actual position of election? Who are involved?
7. What are the criteria that are essential for the candidate who are standing for official posts?
8. Is each office bearer primarily responsible for his specific function?
9. By mutual agreement can they transfer the functions each other?
10. In your association anybody is causally or permanently employed in order to do the work in the association. Yes/No.
    If yes give details.

Activities of the Members, Office Bearers and Meetings

1. What are the types of meetings do you have? How many meetings do you organize monthly, yearly, etc.
2. What is the proportion of members and office bearers attend the meetings?
3. How do you inform your members and office bearers about the meetings and other functions organized by your association?
4. How long members including office bearers spend time in the association beyond attendance and meetings?

5. Did your association arrange any extra associational activities? Yes/No.
   If yes, what sort?
6. Who are all involved in decision-making?

Utility

1. Are the facilities available in the association enjoyed only by the members of the association or also by his family members?
2. Are the members always free to approach the association and make use of their needs? Or are they expected to follow the strict procedure laid down by the association?

Participation

1. Do all members take active participation in the functions organized by the association?
2. Do other community members participate in the functions organized by your associations?
3. Do you expect all the members to participate the common activities of the association?

Economy

1. What is the total annual income of your association?
2. What is the total expenditure of your association per year?
3. Is there any other sources of financial contribution other than membership fee? Yes/No.
   If yes, please specify.
4. Is your association getting any help or financial assistance from your community on government back home or vice-versa.

Publications

1. Whether your association have any publications? If yes give details.

Rules and Regulations

1. Do your association have a written rules and regulations? Yes/No. If yes, specify.

2. Does your community leaders have any authority over this association?
3. What is the official language of your association?
4. Does this association have any symbols or flag of its own?
5. Do you have filing system?

Functions and Activities of the Association

1. Does your association have any social, cultural or public events? If yes list them.
2. Which period would you consider one of the peak periods in the history of the association? As well as worse period.
3. What would you say this organization does it for
   (a) its members
   (b) community as a whole.
4. What would you list as one of the accomplishment of the association?
5. How do the organization changed from the founding date to the present?
6. What would you say have been the main changes in the association over the years?
7. Collect the variation membership fee at different stages of its development.
8. Do you experience any personality clashes among the members and office bearers of the association? If yes for what?
9. Collect the various activities of the association and a detailed function of the association from a historical perspectives.

BIBLIOGRAPHY

Acharya, H., 1969, Social Dynamics of Localism, Regionalism and National Integration, *Quarterly Journal of Indian Studies*, Vol. III, 60-65.

Ames, Michael J., 1969, Modernization and Social Structures : Family, Caste and Class in Jamshedpur, *Economic and Political Weekly*, Vol. IV, (Special Number).

Anderson, Robert., 1971, Voluntary Associations in History, *American Anthropologist*, Vol. 73, No.1.

Anderson, Robert and Gellatin Anderson, 1962, Voluntary Associations Among Ukrainian in France, *Anthropological Quarterly*, 35 : 158-68.

Arnold, M. Rose, 1954, *Theory and Method in Social Science*, The University of Minnesota Press, Minneapolis.

Babchuck, N. and Gordon, C.W., 1959, A Typology of Voluntary Associations, *American Sociological Review*, Vol. 24, No.1.

Banton, M., 1955, *The Coloured Quarter*, London, Jonathan Cape.

Banton, M., 1957, *West African City : A Study of Tribal Life in Free Town*, London, Oxford University Press.

Banton, M., 1968, "Voluntary Associations : Anthropological Aspects", *International Encyclopaedia of the Social Sciences*, Vol. 16, 357-62.

Barnes, T. Sandra, and Peil Margaret, 1977, Voluntary Association Membership in Five West African Cities, *Urban Anthropology*, Vol. 6, No.1.

Blegan, T.C., 1940, *Norwegian Migration to America*, Minnesota.

Borhek, J.T., 1970, Ethnic – Group Cohesion, *American Journal of Sociology*, Vol. 76, No.1.

Buchanan, M.D., Francis, 1807, *Journey from Madras through the Countries of Mysore, Canara and Malabar*, Vol. 1, London.

Clement, Pierre, 1956, "Social effects of Urbanization in Stanleyville, Belgian Congo" in *Social Implications of Urbanization in Africa.* South of the Sahara, Paris, UNESCO.

Cressey, P.F., 1938, Population Succession in Chicago 1893-1930, *American Journal of Sociology*, Vol. 44, No.1, 59-69.

Cutler, S.J., 1973, "Voluntary Association Membership and the Theory of Mass Society" in E.C. Lauman (ed.), *Bonds of Pluralism*, John Wiley and Sons.

Despres, L.A., 1968, Anthropological Theory, Cultural Pluralism, and the Study of Complex Societies, *Current Anthropology*, Vol. 9, No.1, Utrecht Netherlands.

Dewitt, John, 1969, *Indian Worker's Association in Briton*, London, Oxford University Press.

Enthoven, R.E., 1922, *The Tribes and Castes of Bombay*, Vol. II, Printed at the Government Central Press, Bombay.

Etzioni, A., 1959, The Ghetto – A re-evaluation, *Social Forces*, Vol. 37, No.3, 255-62.

Fox, Richard, 1967, "Resiliency and Change in Indian Caste System : The Umar of U.P." *Journal of Asian Studies*, Vol. 26.

Gadgil, D.H., 1945, "Poona : A Socio-Economic Survey", Part I, Economics, Gokhale Institute of Politics and Economics, Publication No.12.

Gadgil, D.R., 1952, "Poona : A Socio-Economic Survey", Part II, Gokhale Institute of Politics and Economics, Publication No.25.

Galitzi, C.A., 1929, *A Study of Assimilation Among the Roumanians in the United States*, Columbia.

Gans, Herbert, 1962, *The Urban Villagers*, New York, The Free Press.

Ghurye, G.S., 1961, *Caste, Class and Occupation* Bombay, Popular Prakashan.

Glass, R., 1960, "New Comers : The West Indians in London", Centre for Urban Studies, Report No.1, (London, C.U.S. and George Allen and Unwin).

Gough, E.K., 1965, "Indian Nationalism and Ethnic Freedom" in Dovid Bidney (ed.) *The Concept of Freedom in Anthropology*, The Hague, Monton.

Gould, H.A., 1963, Adaptive Functions of Caste in Contemporary Indian society, *Asian Survey*, Vol. 3, No.9.

Hardgrave, L. Robert., 1969, *The Nadars of Tamil Nadu The Political Culture of a Community in Change*, University of California Press, Berkeley and Los Angeles.

Hiro, D., 1971, *Black British White British*, London, Eyre and Spottiswoode.

Hunter, Guy, 1963, *New Societies of Tropical Africa*, London, Oxford University Press.

Hutton, J.H., 1946, *Caste in India*, Cambridge University Press.

Hutton, J.H., 1963, *Caste in India : Its Nature, Function and Origins*. Fourth ed., Oxford University Press.

Iravathi L. Ashenna., 1971, *Majha Aaushyantila Tippane* (in Marathi), Sholapur.

Iyyer, L.K., Anantha Krishna and R.V. Manumandayya, 1931, *The Mysore Tribes and Castes*, Vol. IV., Published under Auspices of the Mysore University, Mysore.

Jones, F.L., 1964, Italians in the Carlton Area : the Growth of Ethnic Concentration, *The Australian Journal of Politics and History*, Vol. 10, No.1.

Jongkind, F., 1974, A reappraisal of the Role of the Regional Associations in China, Peru, *Comparative Studies in Society and History*, 14 : 471-482.

Kakade, R.C., 1947, *A Socio-Economic Survey of Weaving Communities in Sholapur*, Gokhale Institute of Politics and Economics Publication No.14.

Kerri, J.N., 1972, An Inductive Examination of Voluntary Association Functions in a Single-Enterprise Based Community, *Journal of Voluntary Action Research*, 1:43-51.

Kerri, J.N., 1974, Anthropological Studies of Voluntary Associations and Voluntary Action – A review, *Journal of Voluntary Action Research*, Vol. 3, No.1, Winter.

Khare, R.S., 1970, *Changing Brahmins : Association and Elites Among Kanyakubjas of North India*, New York, Columbia, University Press.

Kondapi, C., 1951, *Indians Overseas, 1838-1949*, Oxford University Press, Madras.

Kothari, Rajni and Maru Rushikesh, 1965, Caste, and Secularism in India, *Journal of Asian Studies*, Vol. 25.

Kothari, Rajani, 1970, *Politics in India*, Orient Longman, New York.

Lewandowski, Susan, 1980, *Migration and Ethnicity in Urban India : Kerala Migrants in the city of Madras 1870-1970*, Manohar, Delhi.

Little, K., 1957, The Role of Voluntary Associations in West African Urbanization, *American Anthropologist*, Vol. 59, No.4, August, 579-96.

Little, Kenneth, 1965, *West African Urbanization : A Study of Voluntary Association in Social Change*, Cambridge University Press, Cambridge.

Lloyd, I.R., 1965, The Modernity of Tradition : The Democratic Incarnation of Caste in India, *American Political Science Review*, Vol. LIX, No.4, 975-989.

Lloyd, P.C., 1967, The City of Ibandan, P.C. Lloyd, Mabogunje and B.Awe (eds.), Cambridge, Cambridge University Press.

Lloyd, P.C., 1969, *Africa in Social Change: Changing Traditional Societies in the Modern World*, Baltimora : Penguin Books.

MacDonald, J.S., and MacDonald, L.D., 1964, Chain Migration, Ethnic Neighbourhood Formation and Social Networks, *Milbank Memorial Fund Quarterly*, Vol. 42, No.1. 82-97.

Majamdar, D.N., 1958, *Caste and Communication in an Indian Village*, Asia Publishing House, Bombay.

Mangin, W., 1959, The Role of Regional Associations in the Adaptation of Rural Population in Peru, *Sociologus*, 9: 23-36.

Mayer, A.C., 1960, *Caste and Kinship in Central India : A Village and its Region*, London, Routledge and Kegan Paul.

Meillassoux, Claude, 1968, *Urbanization of African Community : Voluntary Associations in Bomako*, Seattle and London : University of Washington.

Nair, K.S., 1978, *Ethnicity and Urbanization*, Ajanta Publications, Delhi.

Nair, K.S., 1983, Structural Pluralism and Ethnic Boundaries: an Empirical Analysis, *Ethnic and Racial Studies*, Vol. 6, No.4.

Norbeck, Edward, 1977, Changing Associations in a Recently Industrialized Japanese Community, *Urban Anthropology*, Vol. 6, No.1.

Ottenberg, S., 1955, Improvement Associations among the Afikpo Ibo, *Africa*, Vol. XXV, No.1.

Park, R.E., 1955, "The Collected Papers of Robert Ezra Park, Vol. III", Society ed. E.C. Hughes et. al Glencoe, III, The Free Press.

Parkin, D., 1966, Urban Voluntary Associations as Institutions of Adaptation, *Man*, 1:90-95.

Plotnicov, Leonard., 1967, *Strangers to the City*, Pittisburgh : University of Pittisburgh Press.

Pradhan, M.C., 1966, *The Political System of the Gats of Northern India*, Oxford University Press.

Price, C.A., 1959, "Immigration and Group Settlement with a Special Reference to European Settlers in Australia, Canada and United States" in Borrie, W.D. (ed.). *The Cultural Integration of Immigrants,* UNESCO.

Price, John, A., 1975, U.S. and Canadian Indian Urban Ethnic Institutions, *Urban Anthropology*, 4(1), 31-52.

Punekar, V., 1974, *Assimilation*, Bombay Popular Prakashan.

Rao, M.S.A. (ed.), 1974, *Urban Sociology in India*, New Delhi, Orient Longmans.

Rao, M.S.A, 1978, "Social Movements Among the Backward Classes and Blacks : Homology in the Sources of Identity" in M.S.A. Rao (ed.) *Social Movements in India*, Vol. I, Manohar, Delhi.

Rowe, L.W., 1973, "Caste Kinship and Association in Urban India", in A. Southall (ed.) *Urban Anthropology*, pp. 211-51, New York : Oxford University Press.

Rudolph, Lloyd, 1965, The Modernity of Traditions : The Democratic Incarnation of Caste in India, *The American Political Reviews*, Vol. LIX, No.4.

Rudolph, Lloyd I and Susan, H., 1960, The Political Role in Indian Caste Association, *Pacific Affairs* 35 : 5-22, No.1.

Saha, Panchanan, 1970, *Emigration of Indian Labour 1834-1900*, Peoples Publishing House, Delhi.

Sangave, Vilas., 1962, Changing Pattern of Caste Organization in Kolhapur City, *Sociological Bulletin*, 11 (1-2), 36-61.

Sheldon, Ronald, 1976, Regional Associations and Population Migration in Peru, *Urban Anthropology*, Vol. 5, No.3.

Singer, Milton, 1959, "The Great Tradition in a Metropolitan Centre : Madras", in Milton Singer (ed.) *Traditional India – Structure and Change*, Philadelphia, The American Folklore Society.

Singer, Milton, 1968, "The Joint Family in the Modern Industry" in Milton Singer and Bernard, S. Cohen (ed.) *Structure and Change in Indian Society*. Aldine Publishing Company.

Singh, Andrea Manefee, 1976, *Neighbourhood and Social Network in Urban India*, Marwah, New Delhi.

Singh, Parmanand, 1982, *Equality, Reservation and Discrimination in India*, Deep and Deep Publications, Delhi.

Singh, Yogendra, 1973, *Modernization of India Tradition*, Thomson Press, (India), Ltd.

Smock, A.C., 1971, *Ibo Politics*, Cambridge Massachusetts, Harvard University Press.

Southall, Adian (ed.). 1961, *Social Change in Modern Africa*, London : Oxford University Press.

Srinivas, M.N., 1954, A Caste Dispute Among the Washerman of Mysore, *Eastern Anthropologist*, Vol. 7, 140-63.

Srinivas, M.N., 1956, A Note on Sanskritisation and Westernisation, *Far Eastern Quarterly*, Vol. IV, No.4.

Srinivas, M.N., 1959, Caste of Potter and the Priest, *Man in India*, Vol. 39, No.3, 199-209.

Srinivas, M.N., 1962, *Caste in Modern India and Other Essays*, Asia Publishing House, Bombay.

Srinivas, M.N., 1972, *Social Change in Modern India* Orient Longman.

Steward, J.H., (ed.), 1967, *Contemporary Change in Traditional Societies*, Vol. I, University of Illinois, Urbana.

Syed Siraj ul Hussan, 1920, "The Caste and Tribes of H.E.H., The Nizam's Dominions", Vol. I, Bombay, *Times of India.*

Tinker, Hugh, 1974, *A New System of Slavery : The Export of Indian Labour Overseas, 1830-1920*, Oxford University Press, London.

Uchendu, V., 1965, *The Lgbo of South East Nigeria*, New York, Holt Rinehard and Wiston.

Vatuk Sylvia, 1972, *Kinship and Urbanization : White Collar Migrants in Northern India*, University of California, London.

Verma, K.K., 1979, *Changing Role of Caste Association* National Publishing House, New Delhi.

Weiner, Myron, 1967, *Segmentation and Political Participation in Khaira District in Party Building in a New Nation*, Chicago University Press, Chicago.

Wirth, L., 1938, Urbanism as a Way of Life, *American Journal of Sociology*, 44 : 1-24.

Wunsch, S. James, 1978, Voluntary Associations and Structural Development in West-African Urbanization, *Journal of African Studies*, Vol. 5, No.1.

Yuzyk, P., 1953, *The Ukranians in Minitoba*, Toronto.

Government of India Publications

Census of India, 1961, Vol. X, Maharashtra, Part II-(1) Social and Cultural Tables, Central Government Publications.

Census of India, 1971, Maharashtra, Part II-C(1) Social and Cultural Tables, Central Government Publications.

Gazetteer of the Bombay Presidency, 1882, Vol. III, Thana Under Government Order, Printed at the Central Press.

Gazetteer of Bombay Presidency, 1886, Poona, Printed at the Government Central Press.

Gazetteer of Bombay State, 1954, (Revised Edition). District Series Vol. XX, Poona District, Bombay Printed at the Government Central Press.

Report of the Backward Classes Commission, 1980, Part I and II, Government of India.

Other Sources

The Telugu Samachar, 1925, Maker Shankranthi Edition, Bombay.

Padmajyoti (Monthly) in Telugu, Published from Hyderabad.

Pakshik Padmasali (Fortnightly), in Telugu and Marathi Published from Nanded, Maharashtra.

INDEX

Acharya, H., 22
Accommodation, 121, 122, 131
Active association, 94, 137
Adult education, 127
Ahmedabad, 148
All India Padmasali Mahasabha, 145, 150, 153, 154
All India Padmasali Women's Mahasabha, 150
Amalgamation, 18
Anderson, Robert, 16
Andhra Pradesh, 37, 149
Andhra Pradesh Cyclone Relief Fund, 108
Andhra Saraswathy Parishad, 131
Anmol, A.N., 123
Arnold, M. Rose, 91
Assimilation model, 174
Authority structure, 58, 80

Backward Class Committee, 29
    movement, 18, 28, 128, 145
    status, 158
Backward Classes Commission, 140, 155, 158, 159
Baji Rao Peshwa, 41
Bal Gangadhar Tilak, 132
Ballot voting, 172
Bangalore, 148
Banton, M., 11
Bhajan Mandals, 104
Bhavanipeth, 48, 97
Bombay, 101
British rule, 138

Calcutta, 101
Camp education society, 42
Caste association, 18
    customs, 163
    panchayats, 34, 55, 57, 89, 119, 128
        classification of, 57, 62
    sabhas, 14, 140, 172
        emergence of, 139
Ceded districts, 41
Chain migration, 19, 173
    settlement, 24
Charitable Trust, 80
Chowdhary, 65, 79
    system, 118
Clement, Pierre, 16
Colonial period, 23, 41
Common fund, 67, 74, 83
Committee meetings, 66, 72, 82
Common property, 67, 74, 83

Communication system, 23
Community welfare associations, 102
Conferences, 147, 148, 155
Contract labourers, 19
Co-operative handloom societies, 101
Co-operative housing societies, 100
Costi famities, 38
Cuddapah, 146
Customs, 143, 150, 162

Dahihandi, 103
Data collection, methods of, 32-34
Deculturation, process of, 135
Dehumanization, 11
Democratization, 27, 57, 58, 172
    levels of, 67, 74, 83
Desanskritisation, 31
Dhobi Dargigalli Tarun Mandal, 99
Dichotomisation, 165
Disbanded associations, 36, 92, 128, 136
Dispersed immigrants, 21
Disputes, 211
Dowry, 150

Education activities, 108
    associations, 94, 112
Endogamy, rules of, 78, 88
Ethnic associations, 15, 19, 28, 138
    changing role of, 30
    classification of, 26, 166, 167, 168
    development of, 92
    segregations, 12
    settlements, 19, 37, 51
    types of, 23-25

Factors, 167
Family planning, 150
Festivals, 127
Financial crisis, 121
First World War, 118, 120
Functions, 112, 115, 123
Funeral ceremonies, 116
Fused panchayats, 57, 86, 90, 166, 171

Gadgil, D.H., 38
Galitzi, C.A., 18
Games and sports, 125, 126
Ganapati, 142
Ganesh festivals, 98, 126, 132
Ganjpeth, 38, 48, 53, 97
General Body meeting, 66, 72
Ghurye, G.S., 14

Gita Granthalaya, 97
Gita Purayan, 145
Goddess Markandeya, 133
Government policy, 31
Group settlement, 19
Gujarat, 149
Gujarat Padmasali Jynata Samastha, 158
Gullollu Community, 115
Gurukul Kangadi, Hardwar, 144
Guy Hunter, 11

Handloom industries, 120, 153
 development of, 154, 161
Hanuman Jayanthi, 103
Hardgrave, L. Robert, 139, 140
Haridwar, 144
Hindu festivals, 80
Hutton, J.H., 55
Hyderabad, 41

Indentured labourers, 19
 migration, 22
Indian urbanization, 173
Individual migration, 173
Industrialization, 15, 25, 26, 51, 55, 94, 109
Informal buffer, 16, 17
Integrative functions, 103
Itzioni, 21
Iyyer, L.K. 142

Janata Party, 158
Joint family, 12
Judicial functions, 65, 71, 81, 116
 system, 55
Jyoti Sangam, 124, 130

Kacha Devayani, 133
Kaka Kalekar, 140
Kamathis, 37
Kammas, 152
Kanchipuram, 147
Kanyakubja Brahmins, 14, 164
Karimnagar, 48
Khare, R.S., 164, 169
Khatris, 38
Kirkee Cantonments areas, 31, 42, 44, 53, 79, 113
Korutta Padmasali Samudhu Jyoti Sangam, 131
Kothari, Rajni, 119
Kruti Samithi, 90
Kshatriya, 139
Kuchan, G.P., 157, 159
Kulagrantha Samskarana Committee, 152

Lewandowski, Susan, 12, 16, 169
Little, Kenneth, 11, 16, 26
Lloyd, I.R., 16
Lloyd, P.C., 169
Lord Surya, 142
Lord Venkateshwara, 108
Lord Wellesley, 41
Lower caste communities, 41, 119, 123

MacDonald, J.S., 20
Madras, 101
 assembly, 147
Maharashtra, 149
Mahasabha, 149
Majumdar, D.N., 55
Managing committee, 13
Mandals, 98, 99, 105
Mandal Commission, 140
 Report, 157-59
Mandal Panchayat, functions of, 116-17
Manad Panchayat, 113, 118
Manadi communities, 113, 115
Mangalgiri, 152
Marathas, 31, 41
Markhandeya Jayanthi, 103
Markhandeya Purana, 152, 153
Marriage, 78, 88
 functions, 117
 regulations of, 65, 70, 81
Mass migration, 18, 173
Medak, 143
Medical facilities, 123, 131
Meillassoux, Claude, 11, 12, 16, 22, 26
Mela, 132
Methodology, 31
Michael, Ames, 12
Migration, 17, 21, 37
Mobility, types of, 31-33
Modern association, 13
 education, 138
 organizations, 165, 166
Munnurwars, 44
Muslims, customs of, 153-54

Nadar Mahajana Sangam, 140, 164
Nair, K.S., 16, 169
Nanapeth, 48, 97
National days, 127
Newspapers, 127
Nizam, 41
Nizam Rashtra Padmasali Mahasabha, 145, 150, 154, 161
Nizamabad, 44, 47, 48, 120
 Sangam, 120, 124, 130
 State, 153
Nyaya committee, 71, 78, 87, 88

Occupation, 141
Organization, levels of, 65, 71, 81
Othenbergh, S., 169

Padmasalis, 47, 48, 49, 54
 aspiration of, 141
Padmasali Bhavanarishi Samaj Seva Sangh, 102
Padmasali communities, 94
 magazine, 147, 149, 160
 mahasabha, 141

migration, 121
Padmasali Mahila Bhajan Mandal, 105
Padmasali Panch Committee, 73, 74, 76, 95, 96, 122, 127
  Purohit Sangh, 144
  Samrat Mandal, 126, 127
  Shikshnotejak Samastha, 96
  Sudarshan Krida Mandal, 125, 126
  Yuvak Mandal, 122, 124
  Yuvak Sangh Mofat Vachanalaya, 124
Panchamahal, 54, 153
Panchayat, 13, 72, 80, 85
  types of, 86
Parvathi Hill, 39
Passive association, 92, 112, 168
Peshwa's rule, 38
Pilgrims, 22
Pochamma worship, 117
Political mobilization, 13, 24, 157
  modernization, 17
Post-colonial period, 25, 50
Pre-colonial period, 21, 37
Price, C.A., 137
Public Trust Act, 98, 115, 166
Pune contonment, 32
Pune Municipal Corporation, 32

Quasi-Participant Observational technique, 35

Rangoli, 85
Rao, M.S.A., 12
Rashtriya Shivan Kala Kamgar Sabha, 102
Recreational activities, 109
Regional association, 106, 109, 172
Regular election, 68, 75
Religious activities, 117
  association, 104, 112
  festivals, celebration of, 120
Reservation facilities, 163
  percentage of, 159
Resolutions, 147, 148, 162
Rishis, 142
Rowe, William, 12
Rudolph, Lloyd, 14, 24, 139
Rural migration, 30

Sabha, 159
Sabha organisation, 150
Samastha Telugu Manad Panchayat, 43, 123
Samrat mandal, 125, 126
Sanjeeva Reddy, N., 126
Sanskritization, 13, 18
Sarvajanik Ganeshostav, 99
Second World War, 50, 18
Shiv Jayanthi, 103
Shramadan, 103
Shukrawar peth, 31, 53
Singer, Milton, 12
Singh, A.M., 12
Singh, Yogendra, 29
Social reform activities, 157
Sodalities, 89
Srinivas, M.N., 14, 28, 55, 139
Srinivas Bhajan Mandal, 105
Syed Husan, 141

Telugu Dhobis, 44
  community, 111
Telugu education fund, 42, 129
Telugu general library, 130
Telugu Hindu Mala Union, 69
Telugu immigrant communities, 33, 34, 49, 99, 167
Telugu language, examination in , 131
Telugu lower caste communities, 44
Telugu Madelwar Community, 79, 133
  panchayat, 75
Telugu migrants, 134
  mochis, 46
  shimps, 44
Telugu Shimpi Samaj, 82, 84
Telugu speaking people, migration of, 37, 41, 119
  settlement of, 53
Tirumala Tirupati Devasthanams (TTD), 107
Traditional Caste Panchayat, characteristics of, 88-89
Traditional association, 169
Transformed association, 36, 92, 124
Transformation, stages of, 124
Transitional authority structures, 70-74
  panchayats, 57, 87
Typology, 55

Uchendu, V., 169
Urban caste panchayat, 59
Urbanization, 11, 15, 21, 23, 25, 55, 91

Vaishyas, 28
Vajpayee, A.B., 158
Vatuk, Sylvia, 12
Vedic Satsang Mandal, 144-45
Verma, K.K., 164, 169
Village, caste panchayat, 58, 59, 116
Voluntary association, characteristics of, 165-66
  proliferation of, 11, 115

Weakers families, classification of, 48
Welfare activities, 103
West African urbanisation, 16
Women Sabhas, 150
Working committee, 148

Yajurveda, 144
Yeshwantrao Holkar, 4
Yogeshwar Swadhyaya Kendra, 144, 145
Youth Associations, 98, 112
  Sabhas, 150
Yuzyk, P., 18